I0007246

AWS Elemental MediaConvert User Guide

A catalogue record for this book is available from the Hong Kong Public Libraries.

Published in Hong Kong by Samurai Media Limited.

Email: info@samuraimedia.org

ISBN 9789888408702

Copyright 2018 Amazon Web Services, Inc. and/or its affiliates.
Minor modifications for publication Copyright 2018 Samurai Media Limited.

This book is licensed under the Creative Commons Attribution-ShareAlike 4.0 International Public License.

Background Cover Image by https://www.flickr.com/people/webtreatsetc/

Contents

What Is AWS Elemental MediaConvert?

AWS Elemental MediaConvert is a file-based video processing service that provides scalable video processing for content owners and distributors with media libraries of any size. AWS Elemental MediaConvert offers advanced features that enable premium content experiences, including:

- professional broadcast codecs that support increased bit depth and HDR content creation
- still graphic overlays
- advanced audio
- digital rights management (DRM)
- closed captioning support

AWS Elemental MediaConvert offers support for various input formats and adaptive bitrate (ABR) packaging output formats for delivering high-quality content from a range of sources onto primary and multiscreen devices.

For simple use cases, you can set up an AWS Elemental MediaConvert transcoding job in just a few steps. For instructions, see Getting Started with AWS Elemental MediaConvert.

AWS Elemental MediaConvert has the following components:

Jobs

A *job* does the work of transcoding. Each job converts an input file into an output file or files. Inputs and outputs can contain one or more of video, audio, and captions, either together or in separate files. Before you begin creating jobs, make sure that you know what your input files are and what they contain. Also make sure that you know what files you would like to create as output and what format you would like them in.

When you create a job, you specify the name of the file that you want to transcode, the names that you want AWS Elemental MediaConvert to give to the finished output files, and several other settings.

Queues

A *queue* allows you to manage the resources that are available to your account for parallel processing of jobs. AWS Elemental MediaConvert processes jobs that are submitted to a queue in parallel until the resources that are available to the account are used. If the account is already using all of its resources, AWS Elemental MediaConvert begins processing the next job in the queue after it finishes one of the jobs that it's currently processing.

All jobs must be submitted to a queue. If you don't specify the queue when you create jobs, AWS Elemental MediaConvert sends them to a default queue and starts them in the order in which you create them.

If you have jobs of differing priorities, you can handle high-priority jobs by creating a different queue from the default queue. This distributes the resources that are available to the account across the two queues. Because jobs across multiple queues are processed in parallel (until the resources that are available to the account are used), you can submit most jobs into the default queue and use the other queue only when you need to transcode a job immediately. It is important to note that creating additional queues does not increase the resources that are available to the account.

The time that is required to complete a job varies significantly based on the size of the file that you're converting and the job specifications. Accordingly, jobs don't necessarily complete in the order in which you create them. You can temporarily stop processing jobs by pausing the queue. AWS Elemental MediaConvert does not process jobs from a paused queue; however, you can still submit jobs to a paused queue. You can also cancel jobs in a queue that have not yet started transcoding.

Presets

A *preset* is a saved group of encoding settings for a single output. You can create many common outputs by simply selecting a system preset. You can also create your own custom presets, either by duplicating and modifying an existing preset or by creating one from scratch.

When you create a job, you can specify a preset you want to use or you can individually specify your encoding settings.

Job templates

A *job template * specifies all the settings for a complete job, except for your IAM role and those settings that are likely to change for each job, such as the input file location and name, and user metadata you might tag the job with. You create a job templates by specifying all input settings other than input location and filename and then specifying all the outputs the job will generate. You can specify the settings for each output by choosing a preset for the output or by specifying each output setting individually.

Getting Started with AWS Elemental MediaConvert

This Getting Started tutorial shows you how to use the AWS Elemental MediaConvert console to transcode media files in a few basic steps. To get started using the API, see the AWS Elemental MediaConvert API Reference.

AWS Elemental MediaConvert takes in an input file and the information that you provide about that file and turns it into one or more output files, based on the instructions and transcoding settings that you provide.

Note
If you aren't familiar with jobs, queues, presets, and job templates—the basic concepts behind AWS Elemental MediaConvert—we recommend that you take a quick look at What Is AWS Elemental MediaConvert? before you begin the tutorial.

- Step 1: Sign Up for AWS
- Step 2: Create Storage for Files
- Step 3: Set Up IAM Permissions
- Step 4: (Optional) Get Set Up to Use Encryption
- Step 5: Upload Files for Transcoding
- Step 6: Create a Job

Step 1: Sign Up for AWS

To use AWS Elemental MediaConvert, you need an AWS account. If you don't already have an account, you are prompted to create one when you sign up. You aren't charged for any AWS services that you sign up for unless you use them.

To sign up for AWS

1. Open https://aws.amazon.com/, and then choose **Create an AWS Account**. **Note** This might be unavailable in your browser if you previously signed into the AWS Management Console. In that case, choose **Sign in to a different account**, and then choose **Create a new AWS account**.

2. Follow the online instructions.

   Part of the sign-up procedure involves receiving a phone call and entering a PIN using the phone keypad.

Step 2: Create Storage for Files

AWS Elemental MediaConvert transcodes your input files to generate output files. For input and output locations, AWS Elemental MediaConvert works with Amazon S3 buckets.

To create an Amazon S3 bucket

1. Sign in to the AWS Management Console and open the Amazon S3 console at https://console.aws.amazon. com/s3/.

2. On the Amazon S3 console, choose **Create bucket**.

3. In the **Create bucket** dialog box, type a bucket name. If you want to create separate input and output buckets, give the bucket an appropriate name that will help you identify it later.

4. Choose a region for your bucket. Make sure that you create your Amazon S3 buckets and do your AWS Elemental MediaConvert transcoding in the same region.

5. Choose **Create**.

6. If you want to create separate buckets for your input files and output files, repeat steps 2 through step 5.

Step 3: Set Up IAM Permissions

To run transcoding jobs with AWS Elemental MediaConvert, first set up an AWS Identity and Access Management (IAM) role to allow AWS Elemental MediaConvert access to your input files and the locations where your output files are stored. If you use DRM, your IAM permissions also allow AWS Elemental MediaConvert to access your encryption keys through API Gateway.

To set up your AWS Elemental MediaConvert role in IAM

1. Sign in to the AWS Management Console and open the IAM console at https://console.aws.amazon.com/iam/.

2. In the navigation pane of the IAM console, choose **Roles**, and then choose **Create role**.

3. Choose the **AWS service** role type, and then choose the **MediaConvert** service.

4. Choose the **MediaConvert** use case for your service. Then choose **Next: Permissions**. The service has already defined the permissions used by the role. These permissions grant AWS Elemental MediaConvert the following permissions:

   - Full access to your Amazon S3 resources

   - API Gateway invoke full access

   The only entity that can assume this role is the AWS Elemental MediaConvert service.

5. Choose **Next: Review**.

6. For **Role name**, type a name that describes the purpose of the role. You might want to begin the name with "MediaConvert" to make it easy to find when you are creating a job.

   Role names must be unique within your AWS account. You can use up to 64 characters that are letters, numbers, or any of the following: + = , . @ - _

   Because various entities might reference the role, you cannot edit the name of the role after it has been created.

7. (Optional) For **Role description**, edit the description for the new service role.

8. Review the role, and then choose **Create role**.

Step 4: (Optional) Get Set Up to Use Encryption

Protect your content from unauthorized use through encryption. Digital rights management (DRM) systems provide keys to AWS Elemental MediaConvert for content encryption, and licenses to supported players for decryption.

To encrypt content, you must have a DRM solution provider. Get set up by working with one of our AWS DRM solution providers. For information, see http://docs.aws.amazon.com/speke/latest/documentation/customer-onboarding.html.

The only exception to this requirement is with the Apple HLS streaming protocol, where you can choose to define your own static keys or to use a DRM provider.

Step 5: Upload Files for Transcoding

To upload files to an S3 bucket

1. In the **Buckets** pane, choose the name of your input bucket.

2. Choose **Upload**.

3. In the **Upload** dialog box, choose **Add files**, and then upload a media file that you want to transcode.

4. Choose **Upload**.

Step 6: Create a Job

A job does the work of transcoding. You specify the name of the file that you want to transcode (the input file), the name that you want AWS Elemental MediaConvert to give the transcoded file, the preset that you want AWS Elemental MediaConvert to use, and a few other settings. AWS Elemental MediaConvert gets the input file from the Amazon S3 location that you specify in your job input settings, transcodes the file, and saves the transcoded file or files in the output location that you specify in the settings of the job output group.

To create a job

1. Open the AWS Elemental MediaConvert console at https://console.aws.amazon.com/mediaconvert.

2. Choose **Get started**.

3. Choose **Create job**.

4. Provide transcode instructions and job settings. For more information, see Setting Up a Job in AWS Elemental MediaConvert.

   Make sure that you pick the same region for your job and your file storage.

5. In the left navigation pane, under **Job settings**, choose **Settings**.

6. In the **Job settings** section of the console, under **IAM role**, choose the role that you created in Step 3 of this tutorial.

7. Choose **Create**.

8. If you don't want to keep the transcoded files that you generate during this tutorial, delete them from Amazon S3 to avoid incurring storage charges.

Setting Up a Job in AWS Elemental MediaConvert

A job does the work of transcoding a media file. When you create a job, you specify the information that AWS Elemental MediaConvert needs to perform the transcode: which file to transcode, what to name the transcoded files, which encoding settings to use, which advanced features to apply, and so on.

You also create output groups and outputs, and then specify the output settings. For information about how different ways of setting up outputs and output groups affects the assets produced by your job, see [ERROR] BAD/MISSING LINK TEXT.

Specify Input Settings

When you set up a job through the AWS Elemental MediaConvert console, you begin with input settings.

To specify the location of your input:

1. On the **Create job** page, under **Input 1**, provide the URI to your input file stored in Amazon S3 .

   If you want to transcode only a portion of this input file, choose **Add input clip** and specify the portion.

2. Specify values for any of the following video selector fields that are applicable to your job.

   If you leave these settings in their default state, you will create a valid job. For more information on individual settings, choose the **Info** link next to the setting.

3. Create audio selectors for any audio assets from the input used in an input. For more information on setting up audio for your job, see Setting Up Audio in AWS Elemental MediaConvert Jobs

4. Create captions selectors for any captions assets from the input used in an output. For more information on setting up captions for your job, see Setting Up Captions in AWS Elemental MediaConvert Jobs

5. To include another input in this job, in the **Job** navigation pane on the left, choose **Add input**.

   For jobs that have multiple input files, the transcoding service creates outputs by concatenating the input files or clips.

Create Output Groups

After specifying your input settings, create output groups. Each output that AWS Elemental MediaConvert creates must reside in an output group. For adaptive bitrate (ABR) output groups, every output in an output group is packaged in the same ABR stack. For file group output groups, each output is a standalone file. For more information on how your choices of output group and outputs within the group affect the assets created by your job, see [ERROR] BAD/MISSING LINK TEXT.

To create an output group:

1. From the **Job** navigation pane on the left, choose the **Add output group**.

2. Choose an output group type, and then choose **Select**.

3. Optionally, provide a name under **Custom group name**. Any name you provide here will appear in the **Job** navigation pane on the left.

4. Under **Destination**, specify the URI for the Amazon S3 location where the trancoding service will store your output files. **Note**
   You can optionally append a basename to your destination URI. The transcoding service will use this basename in conjunction with any name modifier you provide in the individual output settings to create the filename of your final asset.

If you do not provide a basename with your URI, the transcoding service will generate a basename from the Input 1 filename, minus the extension.

5. Specify the values for the encoding settings that apply to the entire output group. These settings vary depending on which type of output group that you select.

You can create multiple output groups and multiple types of output groups. After you create your output groups, set up the individual outputs within each group.

Create Outputs and Specify Output Settings

After creating output groups, set up your outputs within each group. For more information on how your choices of output group and outputs within the group affect the assets created by your job, see [ERROR] BAD/MISSING LINK TEXT. You can set up an output either by selecting a preset, which is a pre-defined set of values for the output settings, or by specifying the settings individually.

To set up the outputs in an output group:

1. Specify a value for **Name modifier** and **Extension** in **Output 1**. When you create an output group, AWS Elemental MediaConvert automatically populates the output group with output 1, so you do not need to explicitly create it.

   The transcoding service will append the name modifier and extension to the basename to generate the filename it gives this output.

2. If one of the predefined groups of settings listed under **Preset** is suitable for your workflow, choose it from the list. If you use a preset, skip the rest of the steps in this procedure.

3. Specify values for the general settings under **Output settings**. Depending on the output group type, these settings may include transport stream settings or other container settings. For more information on individual settings, choose the **Info** link next to the setting.

4. Specify values for the video encoding under **Stream settings**. The video settings are selected by default, so you don't need to explictly choose this group of settings.

   For more information on individual settings, choose the **Info** link next to the setting.

5. Choose **Audio 1** to bring up the group of stream settings for the first audio asset included in this output. For more information on bringing audio from the input to each output, see Setting Up Audio in AWS Elemental MediaConvert Jobs

6. To include captions in the output, choose **Add captions** to bring up a group of captions settings. For more information on setting up captions, see Setting Up Captions in AWS Elemental MediaConvert Jobs

7. If you want more outputs in this output group, choose the **Add output** link under your output group name.

Specify Global Job Settings

Global job settings apply to every output created by the job.

1. In the **Job** navigation pane on the left, under **Job settings**, choose **Settings**.

2. Under **IAM role**, choose an IAM role that has permissions to access the Amazon S3 buckets that hold your input and output files and has a trusted relationship with AWS Elemental MediaConvert. For information on creating this role, see Step 3: Set Up IAM Permissions.

3. Optionally, specify values for the other job settings and enable global processors. For more information on individual settings, choose the **Info** link next to the setting.

Structuring Complex Jobs in AWS Elemental MediaConvert

A single AWS Elemental MediaConvert job can create outputs in the form of a standalone file (for example, an .mp4 file), a set of files for ABR (for example, an HLS package), or combinations of both.

You specify the number and types of files that your job generates by creating outputs within output groups.

The topics in this section explain the relationship between outputs, output groups, and the actual output files that are produced by AWS Elemental MediaConvert.

- How Output Groups Affect Outputs in AWS Elemental MediaConvert
- Including Video, Audio, and Captions in Outputs in AWS Elemental MediaConvert
- HLS Player Version Support

How Output Groups Affect Outputs in AWS Elemental MediaConvert

An AWS Elemental MediaConvert output functions differently depending on which type of output group it is a part of. In a file output group, each output is a standalone file that contains all the video, audio, and captions together. In an HLS, DASH, or Smooth output group, each output is one rendition in the ABR stack.

A single job can generate zero to many standalone files and zero to many HLS, DASH, and Smooth ABR stacks. To create more than one standalone file, add a single file output group to your job and add multiple outputs to that output group. To create more than one ABR stack, add multiple HLS, DASH, or Smooth output groups to your job.

The following example shows how an AWS Elemental MediaConvert job generates two standalone .mp4 files, two HLS ABR stacks, and a DASH ABR stack.

For information about setting up output groups and outputs within your job, see Setting Up a Job in AWS Elemental MediaConvert.

After you create your outputs within the appropriate output groups, use selectors to specify the video, audio, and captions that you want AWS Elemental MediaConvert to include in each output. For more information, see Including Video, Audio, and Captions in Outputs in AWS Elemental MediaConvert.

Including Video, Audio, and Captions in Outputs in AWS Elemental MediaConvert

You use *selectors* to specify whether information (video, audio, or captions) from your input file is included in a given output. A selector is a construct that AWS Elemental MediaConvert uses to group together data from the input. For example, you might put some, but not all, of an input asset's audio tracks into an audio selector.

Creating Selectors (Input)

When you set up your input, you can create audio and captions selectors. To do that, you specify audio tracks and captions that are in your input and provide some basic information about them. For more information, see Specify Input Settings.

You don't need to create a video selector because AWS Elemental MediaConvert automatically generates a video selector based on the video stream in your input. However, you must provide values for the fields of the existing video selector. AWS Elemental MediaConvert doesn't support inputs with multiple video streams, such as Quad 4k.

Using Selectors (Outputs)

When you set up your outputs, you use selectors to specify the elements (video, audio, or captions) from your input to include in each output. An output might or might not include each type of selector. For example, you might create an audio-only output as a standalone file. Or you might create several outputs with the same video, audio, and captions streams for an ABR stack. (In that case, you likely would apply different settings to the same video in the different outputs.)

Outputs as Standalone Files (File Group)

Standalone file outputs are part of a file group output group. For each element (video, audio, or captions) that you specify by using a selector, AWS Elemental MediaConvert includes content in the file that it creates. Settings that you specify in one output for handling a selected element don't apply to that element in other outputs.

Outputs in an ABR Stack (HLS, DASH, Smooth Groups)

ABR outputs are part of an HLS, DASH, or Smooth output group. Except in unusual cases, you set up your ABR output group with a separate output for each element in your ABR stack. That is, one output per video resolution, one output per audio track, and one output per captions language. You specify each video, audio, or captions element to include in the output by using a selector.

In the following illustration, each orange box represents an output within the output group.

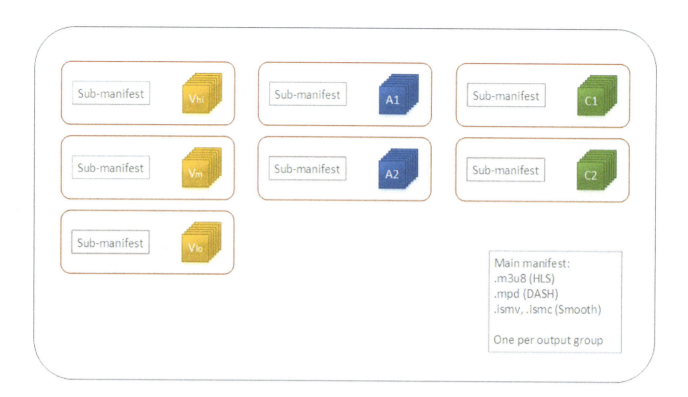

Sub-manifest	Vhi
Sub-manifest	A1
Sub-manifest	C1
Sub-manifest	Vm
Sub-manifest	A2
Sub-manifest	C2
Sub-manifest	Vlo

Main manifest:
.m3u8 (HLS)
.mpd (DASH)
.ismv, .ismc (Smooth)

One per output group

HLS Player Version Support

Most HLS assets that you create with AWS Elemental MediaConvert are compatible with HLS players version 2 and later. Depending on the features that you use in AWS Elemental MediaConvert, some assets require versions of HLS players that are later than version 2, such as versions 3, 4, or 5. AWS Elemental MediaConvert automatically sets the player version metadata based on the features that you enable.

This list shows the features that might require updated player support:

Manifest duration format: HLS output group > Apple HLS group settings > Advanced > Manifest duration format
When you set your manifest duration format to **Integer**, viewers can play the asset with HLS players version 2 and later.
When you set your manifest duration format to **Floating point**, viewers can play the asset with HLS players version 3 and later.

Segment control: HLS output group > Apple HLS group settings > Segment control
When you set segment control to **Single file**, viewers can play the asset with HLS players version 4 and later.
When you set segment control to **Segmented files**, viewers can play the asset with HLS players version 2 and later.

Add I-frame only manifest: HLS Output group > Output > Advanced > Add I-frame only manifest
When you choose **Include**, viewers can play the asset with HLS players version 4 and later.
When you choose **Exclude**, viewers can play the asset with HLS players version 2 and later.

Audio track type: HLS Output group > Output > Output Settings > Advanced > Audio track type
When you choose one of the **Alternate audio** options for any of your audio variants, viewers can play the asset with HLS players version 4 and later.
When you choose **Audio-only variant stream** for **Audio track type** or leave **Audio track type** unselected for all of your audio variants, viewers can play the asset with HLS players version 2 and later.

DRM encryption method: HLS output group > DRM encryption > Encryption method
When you choose **SAMPLE-AES** for **DRM encryption, Encryption method**, viewers can play the asset with HLS players version 5 and later.
When you choose any other value for **DRM encryption, Encryption method**, viewers can play the asset with HLS players version 2 and later.

23

Setting Up Audio in AWS Elemental MediaConvert Jobs

To set up your audio without changing the channels in your tracks, follow the basic steps described in this topic.

For workflows that require channel-level control, use the audio channel remix feature, which supports the following workflows:

- Changing the order of channels in an audio track
- Moving audio channels from one or more input tracks to different output tracks
- Combining the audio from multiple channels into a single channel
- Splitting the audio from a single channel into multiple channels
- Adjusting the loudness level of audio channels

Create Input Audio Selectors

When you set up audio, you begin by creating audio selectors. Audio selectors identify a particular audio track or set of tracks from the input. When you set up an output to include audio, you do so by specifying audio selectors.

To create input audio selectors

1. Open the AWS Elemental MediaConvert console at https://console.aws.amazon.com/mediaconvert.
2. Choose **Create job**.
3. Under **Audio selectors**, under **Selector type**, choose the identifier (track, PID, or language code) that you use to pick the track or set of tracks for this selector.
4. In the field under **Selector type**, specify the track or tracks that you want the encoding service to associate with the selector. You can provide a single value or a comma-separated list of values. You can also use a wildcard (*) instead of a track number.

   For information about the other settings that are available for input audio selectors, choose the **Info** link next to a setting.

5. Create more selectors as necessary. To do so, in the left pane of the **Create new job** page, under **Audio selectors**, choose **Add audio selector** and then specify the tracks that the service will associate with the selector.

Set Up Audio in Outputs

You include audio in your outputs by choosing an audio selector. Create audio selectors before you set up audio in your outputs.

To set up audio for each output

1. Open the AWS Elemental MediaConvert console at https://console.aws.amazon.com/mediaconvert.
2. Follow the steps in Create input audio selectors, and then return to step 3 in this procedure.
3. Set up your input, output groups, and outputs for video and audio, as described in Setting Up a Job in AWS Elemental MediaConvert and Structuring Complex Jobs in AWS Elemental MediaConvert.
4. In the left pane, choose the appropriate output from the list of outputs.
5. Under **Encoding settings**, choose **Audio 1**. This displays an audio settings area.

6. Under **Audio source**, choose an audio selector. This identifies an audio track or set of tracks from the input to include in this output.

7. Choose how you want the audio encoded for the output. For details about each setting, choose the **Info** link next to the setting.

8. Repeat steps 4 through 7 for each output.

About Audio Selectors

You use audio selectors to associate input audio with output audio. You can set up a single audio selector to represent one or more tracks from the input. After that, you create audio tracks in the output and associate a single audio selector with each output track.

Associations between input audio tracks, audio selectors, and output audio tracks follow these rules:

- Each input track can be associated with one or more audio selectors
- Each audio selector has one or more input tracks
- Each output track has one audio selector

The following diagram shows these relationships. In the diagram, the input file contains three audio tracks. Audio selector 1 selects input track 1. Audio selector 1 is associated with output audio track 1, so track 1 of the output has the same content as track 1 of the input. The second input audio track is not selected by an audio selector, so it isn't used in the output. Audio selector 2 selects input tracks 1 and 3. Audio selector 2 is associated with output audio track 2, so output track 2 contains the channels from input tracks 1 and 3.

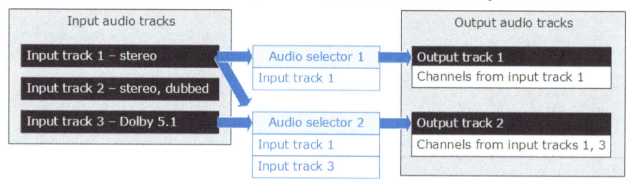

Setting Up Captions in AWS Elemental MediaConvert Jobs

To include captions in your job, follow these steps in the order listed.

- Gather Required Captions Information
- Create Input Captions Selectors
- Set Up Captions in Outputs

Gather Required Captions Information

Before you set up captions in your job, note the following information:

- The *input captions format*. You must have this information ahead of time; AWS Elemental MediaConvert does not read this from your input files.

- The *languages* from the input captions that you intend to use in any of your outputs.

- The *output packages and files* that you intend to create with the job. For information about specifying the output package or file type, see [ERROR] BAD/MISSING LINK TEXT.

- The *output captions format* that you intend to use in each output.

  For supported output captions based on your input container, input captions format, and output container, see Captions Support Tables by Output Container Type.

- The *output captions languages* that you intend to include for each output. If you pass through teletext-to-teletext, all languages in the input are available in the output. Otherwise, the languages that you include in an output might be a subset of the languages that are available on the input.

Create Input Captions Selectors

When you set up captions, you begin by creating captions selectors. Captions selectors identify a particular captions asset on the input and associate a label with it. The captions asset is either a single language or the set of all languages contained in the input file, depending on your input captions format. For example, you might add **Captions selector 1** and associate the French captions with it. When you set up an output to include captions, you do so by specifying captions selectors.

To create input captions selectors

1. On the **Create job** page, in the **Job** pane on the left, choose an input.

2. In the **Captions selectors** section, near the bottom of the page, choose the **Add captions selector** button.

3. Under **Source**, choose the input captions format.

4. For most formats, more fields appear. Specify the values for these fields as described in the topic relating to your input captions format. Choose the appropriate topic from the list following this procedure.

5. Create more captions selectors as necessary. The number of captions selectors you need depends on your input captions format: See the appropriate topic from the list following this procedure.

- QuickTime Captions Track or Captions in MXF VANC Data (Ancillary)
- CEA/EIA-608, CEA/EIA-708 (Embedded)
- DVB-Sub
- Teletext
- SCC, SRT, STL, TTML (Sidecar)

QuickTime Captions Track or Captions in MXF VANC Data (Ancillary)

If your input captions are in either of the following formats, the service handles them as "ancillary" data:

- QuickTime captions track (format QTCC)
- MXF VANC data

AWS Elemental MediaConvert does not create output captions in these formats, but you can convert them to a supported output format.

For ancillary captions

- Create one captions selector per language that you will use in your outputs.

- In each captions selector, for **Source**, choose **Ancillary**.

- In each captions selector, for **CC channel**, choose the channel number for the language that is associated with the selector.

  For example, the input captions have English in CC channel 1 and Spanish in CC channel 2. To use these captions, create Captions selector 1, and then choose 1 in the **CC channel** dropdown list. Next, create Captions selector 2, and then choose 2 in the **CC channel** dropdown list.

CEA/EIA-608, CEA/EIA-708 (Embedded)

If your input captions are in any of the following formats, the service handles them as "embedded":

- CEA-608
- EIA-608
- CEA-708
- EIA-708

Number of Captions Selectors for Embedded Captions

- If all of your output captions are also an embedded format, create only one captions selector, even if you want to include multiple languages in the output. With this setup, AWS Elemental MediaConvert automatically extracts all languages and includes them in the output.
- If all of your outputs are in a format that is not embedded, create one captions selector for each language that you want to include in the output.
- If some of your outputs have captions in an embedded format and some of your outputs have captions in a different format, create one captions selector for the outputs with embedded captions. Also create individual selectors for the outputs with other captions that aren't embedded, one for each language that you want in your outputs.

Captions Selector Fields for Embedded Captions

Source: Choose **Embedded**

CC channel number: This field specifies the language to extract. Complete as follows:

- If you are doing embedded-to-embedded captions (that is, you create only one captions selector for the input embedded captions), AWS Elemental MediaConvert ignores this field, so keep the default value for **CC channel number**.
- If you are converting embedded captions to another format, (that is, you create several captions selectors, one for each language), specify the captions channel number from the input that holds the language that you want. To do that, select the channel number from the dropdown list. For example, select **1** to choose CC1.

Note
AWS Elemental MediaConvert doesn't automatically detect which language is in each channel. You can specify that when you set up the output captions, so that AWS Elemental MediaConvert passes the language code metadata for the captions channel into the output for downstream use.

31

DVB-Sub

AWS Elemental MediaConvert supports DVB-Sub only in TS inputs.

In most cases, create one captions selector per language. In each selector, specify which language you want by providing the PID or language code.

Note
Don't specify the captions in both the **PID** field and the **Language** dropdown list. Specify one or the other.

If you are doing DVB-sub-to-DVB-sub and you want to pass through all the captions languages from the input to the output, create one captions selector for all languages. In this case, keep the **PID **field blank and don't choose any language from the **Language** dropdown list.

Teletext

You can use teletext captions in one of the following ways:

- Teletext can include more data than just captions. If you want to include the entire teletext input, your input and output captions format must be teletext. You can't convert the entire set of teletext data to another captions format.

  AWS Elemental MediaConvert supports teletext-to-teletext only in MPEG-2 outputs.

- You can extract and convert individual captions pages (that is, the captions in a specific language) to another captions format. You can't extract individual captions pages and keep them in teletext format. If you want to extract individual captions pages, you must convert them to another format.

Number of Captions Selectors for Teletext

- If you are doing teletext-to-teletext captions, create only one captions selector, even if you want to include multiple languages in the output. In this case, AWS Elemental MediaConvert automatically extracts all languages and includes them in the output.

- If you are doing teletext-to-other, create one captions selector for each language that you want to include in the output.

- If you are doing teletext-to-teletext in some outputs and teletext-to-other in other outputs, create one captions selector for the teletext-to-teletext, and then create individual selectors for the teletext-to-other, one for each language that AWS Elemental MediaConvert converts.

Captions Selector Fields for Teletext Captions

- **Source**: Choose **Teletext**.
- **Page**: This field specifies the page of the language that you want. Complete as follows:
  - If you are doing teletext-to-teletext captions (that is, you create only one captions selector for the input embedded captions), keep this field blank. AWS Elemental MediaConvert ignores any value that you provide.
  - If you are converting teletext to another format (that is, you create several captions selectors, one for each language), then specify the page for the language that you want. If you keep this field blank, you will get a validation error when you submit the job.

SCC, SRT, STL, TTML (Sidecar)

SCC, SRT, STL, and TTML are sidecar captions formats. With these formats, you provide input captions as a separate file. AWS Elemental MediaConvert handles all sidecar formats the same way. The service can pass them through to the output in the same format or convert them into another sidecar format. In all cases, you must create one captions selector for the entire set of captions languages.

Provide the following values for the captions selector fields:

- **External captions file**: The URI to the captions file. AWS Elemental MediaConvert accepts captions files from Amazon S3.

- **Time delta**: (Optional) Use this setting if you need to adjust the sync between the captions and the video:

  - Type a positive number to add to the times in the captions file. For example, type **15** to add 15 seconds to all the times in the captions file.

  - Type a negative number to subtract from the times in the captions file. For example, type **-5** to subtract 5 seconds from the times in the captions file.

    The format of the times in the captions file doesn't have to match the value in the **Timecode config** field (in the input portion of your job). The number that you type in this field simply delays the captions or makes the captions play earlier, regardless of the timecode formats.

Note

To make sure that your captions are properly synchronized with your video, check that the value for **Timecode source** in the **Video selector** section matches the timecodes in your captions file. For example, if the timecodes in your captions file start at zero but your video has embedded timecodes starting at 01:00:00:00, change the default value for **Timecode source** from **Embedded** to **Start at 0**.

If you use the API or an SDK, you can find this setting in the JSON file of your job, called `TimecodeSource`, located in `Settings`, `Inputs`. When you use SCC, you must provide a value for `TimecodeSource`. Otherwise, AWS Elemental MediaConvert will not insert the captions.

Use Cases for Time Delta

SCC: The start time for the captions is not 00:00:00:00. For captions handling, AWS Elemental MediaConvert always treats the video and audio start time as 00:00:00, even if your input video file has embedded timecodes that start at a time other than 00:00:00:00. If your captions file assumes a start time other than 00:00:00, you might need to adjust the captions start time.

For example, your video file may have embedded timecodes that start at 00:05:00:00 and the first instance of dialogue that requires captions might be one minute into the video, at timecode 00:06:00:00. If your captions file is set to begin captions at 00:06:00:00, you must subtract five minutes from the captions. In this case, you would enter **-300** in the **Time delta** field.

SRT, STL, TTML: The start time in the captions file is slightly off. With these types of captions files, the start time for both the video file (containing video and audio) and the captions file is always 00:00:00.

For example, the first instance of dialogue that requires captions might be at 00:06:15. But in the captions file, this time is marked as 00:06:18 and every other instance of captions is also off by 3 seconds. The solution is to subtract three seconds from the captions file. In this case, you would enter "-3" in the Time delta field.

Set Up Captions in Outputs

The location of the captions in a job depends on your output captions format: your captions might be in the same output as your video, a separate output in the same output group as your video, or in an entirely separate output group. How you set up multiple captions languages also depends on the output captions format. The following procedure shows how to set up captions for different outputs.

To set up captions for different outputs

1. Open the AWS Elemental MediaConvert console at https://console.aws.amazon.com/mediaconvert.

2. Choose **Create new job**.

3. Set up your input, output groups, and outputs for video and audio, as described in Setting Up a Job in AWS Elemental MediaConvert and Structuring Complex Jobs in AWS Elemental MediaConvert.

4. Create input captions selectors as described in [ERROR] BAD/MISSING LINK TEXT.

5. Determine where in your job to specify the captions. This choice depends on the output captions format. Consult the relevant topic below to look this up.

6. In the left pane of the **Create new job** page, choose the appropriate output from the list of outputs.

7. Under **Encoding settings**, choose **Add caption**. This displays a captions settings area under **Encoding settings**.

8. If your output captions format requires a separate group of captions settings for each language in the output, choose **Add captions** again until you have one captions group for each language. To determine whether you need one captions settings group for all languages or one for each language, see the relevant topic below.

9. Under **Encoding settings**, choose **Captions 1** from the list.

10. Under **Captions source**, choose a captions selector. This selects the language or languages that you associated with the selector when you set up your input, so that AWS Elemental MediaConvert will include those captions in this output.

11. Under **Destination type**, choose an output captions format. Check [ERROR] BAD/MISSING LINK TEXT to ensure that you are choosing a supported format.

12. Provide values for any additional fields as described in the relevant topic below.

    - TTML and WebVTT (ABR) Output Captions
    - CEA/EIA-608 and CEA/EIA-708 (Embedded) Output Captions
    - DVB-Sub and Teletext Output Captions
    - SCC, SRT (Sidecar) Output Captions
    - Burn-In Output Captions

TTML and WebVTT (ABR) Output Captions

Where to Specify the Captions

Put your captions in the same output group but a different output from your video.

After you add captions to an output, delete the **Video** and **Audio 1** groups of settings that the service automatically created with the output.

To delete the Video and Audio 1 groups of settings:

1. On the **Create job** page, in the **Job** pane on the left, under **Output groups**, choose the output that contains the groups of setting syou want to delete.

2. The **Video** group of settings is automatically displayed in the **Stream settings** section. Choose the **Remove video** button.

3. The **Audio 1** group of settings is automatically displayed in the **Stream settings** section. Choose the **Remove audio** button.

How to Specify Multiple Languages

Put each captions language in its own output.

CEA/EIA-608 and CEA/EIA-708 (Embedded) Output Captions

Where to Specify the Captions

Put your captions in the same output group and the same output as your video.

How to Specify Multiple Languages

- If your input captions format is embedded (that is, you are passing through embedded-to-embedded), you need to create only one group of captions settings. The captions selector that you choose under **Captions source** includes all languages from the input.

- If your input captions are not embedded, you can only include one captions language per output. In each output, include one group of captions settings. Under **Captions source**, choose the selector that is set up for the language you want to include.

DVB-Sub and Teletext Output Captions

Where to Specify the Captions

Put your captions in the same output group and the same output as your video.

How to Specify Multiple Languages

- If your input captions are the same format as your output captions (passthrough), you need to create only one group of captions settings. The captions selector you choose under **Captions source** includes all languages from the input.

- If your input captions are in a different format, create one group of captions settings for each language. Put each group of captions settings in the same output. They will appear in the list of settings groups as Captions 1, Captions 2, and so forth. In each group of settings, choose the captions selector under **Captions source** that is set up for the language you want to include.

SCC, SRT (Sidecar) Output Captions

Where to Specify the Captions

Put your captions in the same output group but a different output from your video.

After you add captions to an output, delete the **Video** and **Audio 1** groups of settings that the service automatically created with the output.

To delete the Video and Audio 1 groups of settings:

1. On the **Create job** page, in the **Job** pane on the left, under **Output groups**, choose the output that contains the groups of setting syou want to delete.

2. The **Video** group of settings is automatically displayed in the **Stream settings** section. Choose the **Remove video** button.

3. The **Audio 1** group of settings is automatically displayed in the **Stream settings** section. Choose the **Remove audio** button.

How to Specify Multiple Languages

Specify all languages in the same output by creating one group of captions settings for each language. They will appear in the list of settings groups as **Captions 1**, **Captions 2**, and so forth. In each group of settings, choose the captions selector under **Captions source** that is set up for the language that you want to include.

Burn-In Output Captions

Burn-in is a delivery method rather than a captions format. Burn-in writes the captions directly on your video frames, replacing pixels of video content with the captions.

Where to Specify the Captions

Put your captions in the same output group and the same output as your video.

How to Specify Multiple Languages

You can only burn-in only one language of captions.

Working with Queues

You can use queues to manage the resources that are available to your account for parallel processing of jobs. When you create a job, you specify the queue that you want to add the job to. If you don't specify a queue, AWS Elemental MediaConvert puts your job in the default queue. AWS Elemental MediaConvert starts processing the jobs in a queue in the order in which you add them.

One common configuration is to use two queues: the default for standard-priority jobs and a dedicated queue for high-priority jobs. Most jobs go into the default queue. You use the high-priority queue only when you need to transcode a file immediately.

If there are other jobs in a queue when you create a job, AWS Elemental MediaConvert starts processing the new job when resources are available. A queue can process more than one job simultaneously. The time required to complete a job varies significantly based on the size of the file you're converting and the job specifications. As a result, jobs don't necessarily complete in the order in which you create them. You can temporarily pause a queue so that it stops processing jobs. This is useful if you want to cancel one or more jobs, which you can do only before AWS Elemental MediaConvert begins processing the jobs.

- Creating a Queue in AWS Elemental MediaConvert
- Pausing and Reactivating Queues in AWS Elemental MediaConvert
- Listing and Viewing Queues in AWS Elemental MediaConvert
- Deleting an AWS Elemental MediaConvert Queue

Creating a Queue in AWS Elemental MediaConvert

To create a queue

1. Open the AWS Elemental MediaConvert console at https://console.aws.amazon.com/mediaconvert.

2. On the navigation bar of the AWS Elemental MediaConvert console, choose the region that you want to create the queue in. This region is where you create your jobs.

3. In the navigation pane of the console, choose **Queues**.

4. On the **Queues** page, choose **Create new queue**.

5. Type a name and a description for the new queue.

6. Choose **Create queue**.

Pausing and Reactivating Queues in AWS Elemental MediaConvert

If you want to cancel a job, we recommend that you first pause the corresponding queue so that AWS Elemental MediaConvert doesn't start processing the job. After the status of a job changes from **Submitted** to **Progressing**, you can't cancel it.

The following procedure explains how to pause and reactivate a queue by using the console.

To pause or reactivate a queue

1. Open the AWS Elemental MediaConvert console at https://console.aws.amazon.com/mediaconvert.

2. In the navigation pane, choose **Queues**.

3. Select the check box next to the queue that you want to pause or reactivate.

4. Choose **Pause** or **Activate** as applicable.

Listing and Viewing Queues in AWS Elemental MediaConvert

You can list the queues associated with the current AWS account, and you can also view the settings for a specified queue. The following procedure explains how to list queues and how to view settings for a queue by using the AWS Elemental MediaConvert console.

To list queues and view queue settings

1. Open the AWS Elemental MediaConvert console at https://console.aws.amazon.com/mediaconvert.

2. On the navigation bar of the AWS Elemental MediaConvert console, choose the region that you want to list jobs in.

3. In the navigation pane, choose **Queues**. The right pane lists the queues that are associated with the current account.

4. To display detailed information about a queue, choose the arrow next to it.

Deleting an AWS Elemental MediaConvert Queue

Note

You can't delete a queue that contains unprocessed jobs.

To delete a queue

1. Open the AWS Elemental MediaConvert console at https://console.aws.amazon.com/mediaconvert.

2. On the navigation bar, choose the region that contains the queue that you want to delete.

3. In the navigation pane of the console, choose **Queues**.

4. Select the check box for the queue that you want to delete.

5. Choose **Remove**.

Setting Up Timecodes

AWS Elemental MediaConvert manages transcoded video frames by their timecode. The service uses the timecode to synchronize some audio and captions, and to determine the timing for displaying video frames in an output. The service also relies on timecodes to manage features—such as input clipping and graphic overlay (image inserter)—that are applied to only some parts of the video.

There are three distinct groups of timecode settings, located in three different places on the console:

Job-wide timecode configuration
The **Timecode configuration** settings under **Job settings** affect how timecodes appear in the outputs. The settings also affect the system behavior for features that apply to every output in the job. This includes the following:

- The length of time that overlaid graphics (inserted images) remain on the screen

- How your HLS variant playlists show time

- How inserted timecodes appear in your output

- How the service interprets the timecode that you provide if you specify an anchor timecode If you use the API or an SDK, you can find these settings in the JSON file of your job. These settings are under `Settings`, `TimecodeConfig`.

Input timecode setting
The **Timecode source** setting under **Input** affects only the following:

- Synchronization for audio and captions that you provide as input files that are separate from the video

- How the service interprets the timecodes that you provide if you use input clipping to specify only a portion of your input for transcoding If you use the API or an SDK, you can find this setting in the JSON file of your job, called `TimecodeSource`, located in `Settings`, `Inputs`.

Output timecode settings
The timecode settings under **Output** determine whether and how timecode information appears in each output:

- The **Timecode insertion** setting under **Output**, **Stream settings**, **Video** determines whether the service embeds timecode metadata in a given output. You can insert timecodes into MPEG-2, Apple ProRes, H.264, and H.265 outputs.

- The **Timecode burn-in** settings under **Output**, **Stream settings**, **Video**, **Preprocessors** determine whether the service inscribes the timecode visually on the video frame.

To provide frame accuracy, AWS Elemental MediaConvert uses timecodes that specify frames by frame number, not by millisecond. All timecodes are in the following 24-hour format with a frame number: HH:MM:SS:FF.

- Adjusting the Job-wide Timecode Configuration
- Adjusting the Input Timecode Setting
- Adjusting the Output Timecode Settings

Adjusting the Job-wide Timecode Configuration

You can set up your timecode configuration under job settings. These settings affect graphic overlay duration, how time is displayed in HLS variant playlists, and how inserted timecodes appear in the output metadata. They don't affect input clipping or caption and audio synchronization.

To adjust the job-wide timecode configuration

1. On the **Create job** page, in the **Job** pane on the left, choose **Settings**.

2. In the **Timecode configuration** section, for **Source**, choose one of the following values:

- **Embedded**: The service uses any timecodes that are embedded in the video.

- **Start at 0**: The service ignores any embedded timecodes and assigns the first video frame the timecode 00:00:00:00 (HH:MM:SS:FF).

- **Specified start**: The service ignores any embedded timecodes and assigns the first video frame the value that you provide for **Start Timecode**.

   The **Start Timecode** field appears when you choose **Specified start**.

If you use the API or an SDK, you can find this setting in the JSON file of your job, called `Source`, located inside `Settings`, `TimecodeConfig`.

If you don't choose a value for **Source**, the service defaults to **Embedded**. If there are no embedded timecodes, the service sets the timecode of the first frame to zero.

1. Set a value for **Anchor Timecode**.

   If you use an editing platform that relies on an anchor timecode, use **Anchor timecode** to specify a point at which the input and output frames have the same timecode. Use the following 24-hour format with a frame number: HH:MM:SS:FF. This setting ignores framerate conversion.

   The system behavior for **Anchor timecode** varies depending on your setting for **Source**:

   - If you choose **Start at 0** for **Source**, the anchor frame is the timecode that you provide in **Anchor timecode**, counting from 00:00:00:00.

      For example, if you set **Anchor timecode** to 01:00:05:00, the anchor frame is one hour and five seconds into the video.

   - If you choose **Embedded** for **Source**, the anchor frame is the timecode that you provide in **Anchor timecode**, counting from the first embedded timecode.

      For example, if your embedded timecodes start at 01:00:00:00 and you set **Anchor timecode** to 01:00:05:00, the anchor frame is five seconds into the video.

   - If you choose **Specified start** for **Source**, the anchor frame is the timecode that you provide in **Anchor timecode**, counting from the timecode that you specify for the first frame.

      For example, if you specify 00:30:00:00 as your start timecode and you set **Anchor timecode** to 01:00:05:00, the anchor frame is thirty minutes and five seconds into the video.

   If you use the API or an SDK, you can find this setting in the JSON file of your job, called `Anchor`, located in `Settings`, `TimecodeConfig`.

   If you don't set a value for **Anchor timecode**, the service doesn't use any anchor timecode.

2. Under **Timestamp offset**, provide a date. This setting applies only to outputs that support a program-date-time stamp. Use **Timestamp offset** to overwrite the timecode date without affecting the time and frame number. This setting has no effect unless you also include the program-date-time stamp in the output.

If you use the API or an SDK, you can find this setting in the JSON file of your job, called `TimestampOffset`, located in `Settings`, `TimecodeConfig`.

Adjusting the Input Timecode Setting

The value for **Timecode source** that you specify in the input settings affects how the service synchronizes audio and captions that you provide in a file that is separate from the video. It also affects how the service interprets the timecodes that you provide for input clipping. For information about input clipping, see [ERROR] BAD/MISSING LINK TEXT.

To adjust the Timecode source setting

1. On the **Create job** page, in the **Job** pane on the left, choose an input.

2. Under **Video selector**, **Timecode source**, specify whether AWS Elemental MediaConvert reads timecodes from the input or generates them starting from zero. Options are as follows:

   - **Embedded**: The service uses any timecodes embedded in the input video. This is the default value.

     If there are no embedded timecodes in the input, the service behaves as though **Timecode source** were set to **Start at 0**.

   - **Start at 0**: The service sets the timecode of the first frame of the job to 00:00:00:00.

   - **Specified start**: Do not use this option.

   Regardless of the source, timecodes are in the following 24-hour format with a frame number: HH:MM:SS:FF.

   If you use the API or an SDK, you can find this setting in the JSON file of your job, called `TimecodeSource`, located in `Settings`, `Inputs`.

Adjusting the Output Timecode Settings

There are two timecode-related settings that you can adjust differently for each output. These are **Timecode insertion** and **Timecode burn-in**.

Inserting Timecode Metadata

The **Timecode insertion** setting determines whether a given output has timecodes embedded in its metadata. AWS Elemental MediaConvert automatically puts this information in the appropriate place, depending on the output codec. For MPEG-2 and QuickTime codecs, such as Apple ProRes, the service inserts the timecodes in the video I-frame metadata. For H.265 (HEVC) and H.264 (AVC), the service inserts the timecodes in the supplemental enhancement information (SEI) picture timing message.

To include timecode metadata in an output

1. On the **Create job** page, in the **Job** pane on the left, choose an output.

2. Under **Stream settings**, **Timecode insertion**, choose **PIC_TIMING_SEI** to include timecode metadata. Choose **Disabled** to leave out timecode metadata.

If you use the API or an SDK, you can find this setting in the JSON file of your job, called `TimecodeInsertion`, located in `Settings`, `OutputGroups`, `Outputs`, `VideoDescription`.

Burning In Timecodes on the Video Frames

The **Timecode burn-in** setting determines whether a given output has visible timecodes inscribed into the video frames themselves. The timecodes are not an overlay, but rather a permanent part of the video frames.

To burn in timecodes in an output

1. On the **Create job** page, in the **Job** pane on the left, choose an output.

2. Under **Stream settings**, **Preprocessors**, choose **Timecode burn-in**.

3. Optionally, provide values for the **Prefix**, **Font size**, and **Position** settings. Even if you don't provide these values, timecodes are burned into your output using these default values:

   - **Prefix**: no prefix
   - **Font size**: Extra Small (10)
   - **Position**: Top Center

   For details about each of these settings, choose the **Info** link next to **Timecode burn-in**.

If you use the API or an SDK, you can find these settings in the JSON file of your job. These settings are under `Settings`, `OutputGroups`, `Outputs`, `VideoDescription`, `VideoPreprocessors`, `TimecodeBurnin`.

Including SCTE-35 Markers in AWS Elemental MediaConvert Outputs

In a transport stream asset, SCTE-35 markers indicate where downstream systems can insert other content (usually advertisements or local programs). In HLS outputs, the manifest might contain SCTE-35 metadata as well.

With this feature, you have three options:

- Pass markers through from the input to the output.

- Include SCTE-35 information in your HLS manifest.

- Blank out content during ad avails.

By default, the service removes SCTE-35 markers from the output, and therefore doesn't include SCTE-35 information in HLS manifests or do ad avail blanking.

Note
AWS Elemental MediaConvert does not process information from input manifests.

Including SCTE-35 Markers in an Output

You can include any SCTE-35 markers from your input in any output that has an MPEG-2 container. These outputs might be in an HLS package or they might be standalone files.

To pass through SCTE-35 markers from the input to an output:

1. Open the AWS Elemental MediaConvert console at https://console.aws.amazon.com/mediaconvert.

2. Choose **Create new job**.

3. Set up your input, output groups, and outputs for video and audio, as described in Setting Up a Job in AWS Elemental MediaConvert and Structuring Complex Jobs in AWS Elemental MediaConvert. **Note** SCTE-35 markers are only present in transport stream inputs, such as MPEG-2 files. You can only include them in MPEG-2 container outputs. These outputs can be either standalone files or part of an HLS package.

4. Choose an output under either **File group** or **Apple HLS**.

5. Under **Container settings** (for **File group** outputs) or **Transport stream settings** (for **Apple HLS** outputs), find **SCTE-35 source** and choose **Passthrough**.

6. Optionally, under **SCTE-35 PID**, enter a different value from the default **500**.

   A PID, or packet identifier, is an identifier for a set of data in an MPEG-2 transport stream container. PIDs are used by downstream systems and players to locate specific information in the container.

Including SCTE-35 Information in Your HLS Manifest

For outputs in an HLS package, you can have the service include information in the HLS manifest about the SCTE-35 markers that are in each of the outputs.

To include SCTE-35 information in your HLS manifest:

1. Open the AWS Elemental MediaConvert console at https://console.aws.amazon.com/mediaconvert.

2. Choose **Create new job**.

3. Set up your input, output groups, and outputs for video and audio, as described in Setting Up a Job in AWS Elemental MediaConvert and Structuring Complex Jobs in AWS Elemental MediaConvert.

4. Under **Output groups**, choose **Apple HLS**. **Note**
   Your outputs must be in an Apple HLS Output group if you want to include SCTE-35 information in an HLS manifest.

5. Choose **Advanced**.

6. Under **Ad markers**, enable either **AWS Elemental**, **SCTE-35 enhanced**, or both. Use AWS Elemental ad markers if you plan to send use this output with other AWS Elemental media services.

Blanking Out Content from Ad Avails

You can enable Ad avail blanking to remove video content, remove any captions, and mute audio during the portions of the output that are marked as available for ads (ad avails).

You set up whether there are SCTE-35 markers for each output individually, but you enable or disable Ad avail blanking for every output in the job. For the service to blank out portions of the output, you have to both pass through the markers and enable Ad avail blanking.

To enable Ad avail blanking:

1. Create a job and set up outputs to include SCTE-35 markers as described in [ERROR] BAD/MISSING LINK TEXT.

2. In the left navigation pane, under **Job settings**, choose **Settings**.

3. Under **Global processors**, enable **Ad avail blanking**.

4. Optionally, under **Blanking image**, provide a URI to an image file located in an Amazon S3 bucket. If you specify an image here, the service will insert the image on all video frames inside the ad avail. If you don't specify an image, the service will use a black slate instead.

   Blanking images must be .png or .bmp files that are the same size or smaller, in pixels, as the output video resolution.

Using Encryption in AWS Elemental MediaConvert

Protect your content from unauthorized use through encryption. Digital rights management (DRM) systems provide keys to AWS Elemental MediaConvert for content encryption, and licenses to supported players for decryption.

Note
To encrypt content, you must have a DRM solution provider. Get set up by working with one of our AWS DRM solution providers. For information, see http://docs.aws.amazon.com/speke/latest/documentation/customer-onboarding.html.
The only exception to this requirement is with the Apple HLS streaming protocol, where you can choose to define your own static keys or to use a DRM provider.

- Encrypting Content
- SPEKE Encryption Parameters
- Static Key Encryption Parameters
- Troubleshooting Encryption

Encrypting Content

Use the following procedure to enable content encryption in **DASH ISO**, **MS Smooth**, and **Apple HLS** output groups. To use this procedure, you should be comfortable working with output groups. For more information, see [ERROR] BAD/MISSING LINK TEXT.

To encrypt content

1. Open the AWS Elemental MediaConvert console at https://console.aws.amazon.com/mediaconvert.

2. In the navigation pane, under **Output groups**, choose the output group that you want to enable encryption for.

3. Below the main panel, locate and enable the **DRM Encryption** option.

4. Follow one of these two paths, depending on your output group type:

    - For **DASH ISO** and **MS Smooth**, fill in the encryption parameter fields. For more information, see [ERROR] BAD/MISSING LINK TEXT.

    - For **Apple HLS**, fill in the following parameters:

        1. **Encryption method** – Choose **Sample-AES** for Apple HLS Fairplay or **AES-128** for Apple HLS AES-128.

        2. **Key provider type** – Choose **SPEKE** to encrypt using a key provided by your DRM solution provider, or choose **Static Key** to type your own key.

            - For **SPEKE**, fill in the encryption parameter fields. For more information, see [ERROR] BAD/MISSING LINK TEXT.

            - For **Static Key**, see [ERROR] BAD/MISSING LINK TEXT.

SPEKE Encryption Parameters

When you request encryption, you provide input parameters that allow the service to locate your DRM solution provider's key server, to authenticate you as a user, and to request the proper encoding keys. This section describes the options. Some options are available only for particular streaming protocols.

- **Resource ID** – Identifier that you define for the content, which is sent to the key server to identify the current endpoint. How unique you make this depends on how fine-grained you want access controls to be. The service does not allow you to use the same ID for two simultaneous encryption processes.

  The following example shows a resource ID:

```
1  MovieNight20171126093045
```

- **System IDs** – Unique identifiers for your streaming protocol and DRM system. Provide up to two IDs for DASH and exactly one for the other streaming protocols. If you provide more than one system ID, enter them on separate lines, and do not separate them with commas or any other punctuation. For a list of common system IDs, see DASH-IF System IDs. If you do not know your IDs, ask your DRM solution provider.

- **URL** – The URL from the API Gateway proxy that you set up to talk to your key server.

  The following example shows a URL:

```
1  https://1wm2dx1f33.execute-api.us-west-2.amazonaws.com/SpekeSample/copyProtection
```

Additional Configuration Options for Apple HLS

- **(Optional) Constant initialization vector** – A 128-bit, 16-byte hex value represented by a 32-character string that is used with the key for encrypting content.

Static Key Encryption Parameters

The following options are for static key encryption:

- **Static key value** – A valid string for encrypting content.
- **URL** – The URL to include in the manifest so that content can be decrypted.

Troubleshooting Encryption

If the DRM system key server is unavailable when AWS Elemental MediaConvert requests keys, the console displays the following message: Key Server Unavailable

Please have the following information available when contacting a support technician for troubleshooting purposes:

- The region the job was run in
- Job ID
- Account ID
- The name of your DRM solution provider
- Any other details about the problem that you are having that might assist with troubleshooting

Setting Up a Job for HDR

AWS Elemental MediaConvert ingests and outputs video in the following HDR formats:

- HDR10 (rec. 2020 color space)
- HLG (rec. 2020 color space)

and the following standard formats:

- SDR (rec. 609 color space)
- SDR (rec. 709 color space)

AWS Elemental MediaConvert supports HDR with HEVC video assets in transport stream and DASH outputs.

You can create HDR output in the following ways:

- Ingesting HDR content and outputting video in the same format.
- Ingesting HDR content in one format and converting it to the other HDR format. This process changes the video itself and automatically converts the metadata to match the content conversion.
- Ingesting SDR content and converting the color space to an HDR format. This process creates output that is formatted as HDR and automatically converts the metadata to match. **Note**
  This process doesn't upgrade the dynamic range of the video content itself. Therefore, the output is formatted as HDR but looks the same as it would if you created it as an SDR output.

You can't convert HDR video to SDR with AWS Elemental MediaConvert.

With HDR10 outputs, you handle color space metadata by passing through from the input, adding missing data, or correcting inaccurate data.

AWS Elemental MediaConvert automatically reads HDR metadata from the video source.

Color Space Metadata Settings

By default, AWS Elemental MediaConvert sets your color space to **Follow**, which means that your output color space is the same as your input color space, even if the color space changes over the course of the video.

Use the following checklist to modify the color space settings for your job.

Color correction task	How to do it
Replace any missing or inaccurate color space metadata in the input.	[ERROR] BAD/MISSING LINK TEXT
Configure each output stream to include or exclude color metadata as needed.	[ERROR] BAD/MISSING LINK TEXT
Apply color correction as needed in each output stream's preprocessors color correction selections.	[ERROR] BAD/MISSING LINK TEXT

Correcting Input Color Space Metadata

Use the video selector controls to correct for inaccurate or missing color space metadata in your input stream. These settings apply to all output.

Under **Input**, **Video selector**, set the following:

- **Color space** – Choose the proper color space. This must be something other than the **Follow** setting.

- Under Color space usage, choose Force.

- If you choose color space **HDR 10**, under **HDR master display information**, enter your values.

Inserting Color Metadata in the Output

Insert color metadata into each output stream where you need it and disable insertion where you don't need it. To do this, in the output's stream settings, toggle the **Insert color metadata** check box.

Note
Depending on the output type, you might need to choose the output's **More Settings** option to reveal the insert color metadata check box.

Correcting Color in the Output

Set color correction as needed in each output stream's preprocessor settings. By default, AWS Elemental MediaConvert doesn't apply color correction.

In the output's stream preprocessors options, choose **Color corrector**. Enter your values in the selections that appear.

Note

Depending on the output type, you might need to choose the output's **More settings** options to display the preprocessors settings area.

AWS Elemental MediaConvert calculates color correction using the values in these fields combined with the color metadata from the input.

Brightness, Contrast, Hue, and Saturation

Enter correction values as needed for brightness, contrast, hue, and saturation. AWS Elemental MediaConvert uses these settings to apply color correction independent of the other color corrector settings.

Color Space Conversion

Set color space conversion to encode the output stream with a different standard than the input stream. Select the option for the format that you want to convert to. The format that you convert from is determined by the input.

Supported Conversion Options

AWS Elemental MediaConvert supports HDR formats, HDR 10 and HLG 2020, and SDR color spaces, Rec. 601 and Rec. 709, for input and output. Your input color space is set by the input video or by your override of the input video setting. For more information, see [ERROR] BAD/MISSING LINK TEXT.

You can't convert from HDR input to SDR output, but all other conversion options are valid.

The following lists the valid conversion options:

- From any HDR format to any other HDR format (HDR 10 or HLG 2020)

- From any SDR color space to any other SDR color space (rec. 601 and rec. 709)

- From any SDR color space to any HDR format

HDR Master Display

The HDR master display information fields appear when you choose the color space conversion, Force HDR 10. Use these fields to supply master display information metadata to be included in the output.

Including Graphic Overlays with AWS Elemental MediaConvert Image Inserter

The image inserter (graphic overlay) feature lets you insert an image (a BMP, PNG, or TGA file) at a specified time and display it as an overlay on the underlying video for a specified duration. This feature includes fade-in and fade-out capability and adjustable opacity. You can include up to eight overlays in an output.

For example, you might include a logo in the corner of the video frame throughout the duration of the file and an HDR indicator for only the portions of the file that are HDR.

Requirements for the Overlay File

Set up the image files that you want to insert over your video as follows:

- **File type**: Use .bmp, .png, or .tga
- **Aspect ratio**: Use any aspect ratio; it doesn't need to match the aspect ratio of the underlying video.
- **Size in pixels**: Use any size, up to the size of the underlying video. **Note**
  In jobs that scale the video resolution (that is, the size of the video frame), the overlaid image is not scaled. Make sure that the image that you select is scaled to suit the size of the video frame after scaling.

Setting Up Image Insertion

You set up image insertion individually in each output where you want the service to overlay graphics on your video.

To insert an image over your video

1. Open the AWS Elemental MediaConvert console at https://console.aws.amazon.com/mediaconvert.
2. Set up your output groups and outputs for video and audio, as described in Setting Up a Job in AWS Elemental MediaConvert and Structuring Complex Jobs in AWS Elemental MediaConvert.
3. In the left pane of the **Create job** page, choose the appropriate output from the list of outputs.
4. Under **Encoding** settings, under the **Video** tab, find the **Preprocessors** section.
5. Choose **Image inserter**. This displays an **Add image** button.
6. Choose **Add image**.
7. Specify the location of your overlay image and values for the settings to control how the overlay appears on the video. For details about each setting, choose the **Info** link next to the setting.
8. Repeat steps 6 and 7 to add any additional images that you want to include in this output.
9. Repeat steps 3 through 8 for each output that you want AWS Elemental MediaConvert to overlay graphics on.

About Multiple Overlays

You can set up an output with multiple overlay images. Each overlay is independent of the others, with its own settings for opacity, fade-in and fade-out times, position on the frame, and the length of time that it is on the video. You can set up overlays so that they all appear on the underlying video at the same time and physically overlap each other.

If you position overlay images so that they overlap, AWS Elemental MediaConvert layers them according to the value that you provide for the **Layer** setting. The service overlays graphics with higher values for **Layer** on top of overlays with lower values for **Layer**.

.

Transcoding Only a Portion of Your Input (Input Clipping)

You can select portions of your input file (clips) to transcode to your outputs, excluding the rest of the input file. When you create clips for a job, AWS Elemental MediaConvert includes the same clips in every output of the job. If you want two outputs with different clips of the same input file, you must create two jobs and specify different input clips.

Note
To join more than one input file into a single output (input stitching), add another input to the job. You can have up to 50 inputs in a job.
On the **Create job** page, in the **Job** section,, next to **Inputs**, choose **Add**. AWS Elemental MediaConvert stitches together the inputs in the order that you add them.

To set up input clipping

1. On the **Create job** page, in the **Job** pane on the left, choose an input.

2. In the **Input clips** section, choose **Add input clip**.

3. Enter the starting and ending timecodes for the first clip that you want to include. the following 24-hour format with a frame number: HH:MM:SS:FF.

   Make sure that you provide timecodes that make sense with your input timecodes. For example, if your input video has embedded timecodes that start at 01:00:00:00, you would define the start timecode for a clip thirty seconds in as 01:00:30:00, not 00:00:30:00.

4. If your input doesn't have embedded timecodes, change the value of the **Timecode source** for the input. In the **Video selector** section, under **Timecode source**, choose **Start at 0**. Note
   If you change the value of **Source** in the **Timecode configuration** section of the job settings (by choosing **Job Settings** in the **Job** pane), it won't affect input clipping. This setting instead affects how your output timecodes appear and how your audio and some captions formats are synchronized.

5. Specify any additional clips by repeating steps 2 through 4 of this procedure. Multiple clips can't overlap; each **Start timecode** must come after the previous clip's **End timecode**.

   If you specify more than one input clip, they all appear in the output, one after the other, in the order that you specify them.

Supported Input Codecs and Containers

AWS Elemental MediaConvert accepts input files in the following combinations of codecs and containers.

Video

Supported video input codecs and containers are listed in the table below.

Container	Video Codecs Supported with Container
No Container	DV/DVCPRO, AVC (H.264), HEVC (H.265), MPEG-1, MPEG-2
Audio Video Interleave	Uncompressed, DivX/Xvid, DV/DVCPRO
Adobe® Flash®	Flash® 9 File, H.263, AVC (H.264)
Matroska	AVC (H.264), MPEG-2, MPEG-4 part 2, VC-1
MPEG Transport Streams	AVC (H.264), HEVC (H.265), MPEG-2, VC-1
MPEG-1 System Streams	MPEG-1, MPEG-2
MPEG-4	Uncompressed, AVC Intra 50/100, DivX/Xvid, H.261, H.262, H.263, AVC (H.264), HEVC (H.265), JPEG 2000, MJPEG, MPEG-2, MPEG-4 part 2, VC-1
MXF	Uncompressed, AVC Intra 50/100, DNxHD, DV/DVCPRO, DV25, DV50, DVCPro HD, AVC (H.264), JPEG 2000, MPEG-2, Panasonic P2, SonyXDCam, SonyXDCam MPEG-4 Proxy
QuickTime®	Uncompressed, Apple ProRes, AVC Intra 50/100, DivX/Xvid, DV/DVCPRO, H.261, H.262, H.263, AVC (H.264) JPEG 2000, MJPEG, MPEG-2, MPEG-4 part 2
WMV/ASF	VC-1

Audio

Supported audio input codecs and containers are listed in the table below.

Container	Audio Codecs
No Container	
Audio Video Interleave	Dolby® Digital, Dolby® Digital Plus™, Dolby® E frames carried in PCM streams, MPEG Audio, PCM
Adobe® Flash®	AAC
Matroska	AAC, Dolby® Digital, Dolby® Digital Plus™, WMA, WMA2
MPEG Transport Streams	AAC, AIFF, Dolby® Digital, Dolby® Digital Plus™, Dolby® E frames carried in PCM streams, MPEG Audio, PCM, WMA, WMA2
MPEG-1 System Streams	AAC, AIFF, Dolby® Digital, Dolby® Digital Plus™, MPEG, Audio PCM

Container	Audio Codecs
MPEG-4	AAC, Dolby® Digital, Dolby® Digital Plus™, PCM, WMA, WMA2
MXF	AAC, AIFF, Dolby® E frames carried in PCM streams, MPEG Audio, PCM
QuickTime®	AAC
WMV/ASF	WMA, WMA2

Supported Output Codecs and Containers

AWS Elemental MediaConvert supports the following combinations of codecs and containers.

Video

Container	Codecs Supported with Container
MPEG DASH	AVC (H.264), HEVC (H.265)
MPEG-2 TS	AVC (H.264), HEVC (H.265), MPEG-2
HLS	AVC (H.264), HEVC (H.265)
Smooth (ISMV)	AVC (H.264)
MPEG-4 (.mp4)	AVC (H.264), HEVC (H.265)
MPEG-4 Flash (.f4v)	AVC (H.264)
QuickTime	AVC (H.264), MPEG-2, Apple ProRes (with AIFF audio only)
XDCAM	MPEG-2
Raw (no container)	AVC (H.264), HEVC (H.265), MPEG-2

Audio

Supported audio output codecs and containers are listed in the table below.

Container	Codecs Supported with Container
MPEG DASH	Dolby Digital Plus, Dolby Digital, AAC
MPEG-2 TS	Dolby Digital Plus, Dolby Digital, AAC
HLS	Dolby Digital Plus, Dolby Digital, AAC
Smooth (ISMV	Dolby Digital Plus, Dolby Digital, AAC
MPEG-4 (.mp4)	Dolby Digital Plus, Dolby Digital, AAC
MPEG-4 Flash (.f4v)	AAC
QuickTime	Dolby Digital Plus (with H.264 and MPEG-2), Dolby Digital (with H.264 and MPEG-2), AAC (with H.264 and MPEG-2), WAV (with H.264 and MPEG-2), AIFF (with Apple ProRes)
XDCAM	WAV
Raw (no container)	AAC, WAV
Audio Only	
Audio Only MPEG-4	AAC

Captions Support Tables by Output Container Type

- DASH Output Container
- HLS Output Container
- MS Smooth (MSS) Output Container
- MP4 Output Container
- MPEG2-TS File Output Container
- QuickTime Output Container
- No Output Container

DASH Output Container

The following table lists supported output caption formats for this output container, sorted by the input caption container and input caption format.

Embedded captions formats include:

- CEA-608

- EIA-608

- CEA-708

- EIA-708

Ancillary captions include:

- Captions in the Quicktime Captions Track

- Captions in the MXF container VANC data

Input Caption Container	Input Caption Format	Supported Output Caption Formats
MP4 Container	Embedded	Burn inTTML
MXF Container	Embedded	Burn inTTML
	Ancillary	Burn inTTML
	Teletext	Burn inTTML
QuickTime Container	Embedded	Burn inTTML
	Ancillary	Burn inTTML
Raw Container	SRT	Burn inTTML
	TTML	Burn inTTML
	STL	Burn inTTML
	SCC	Burn inTTML
MPEG2-TS Container	Embedded	Burn inTTML
	Teletext	Burn inTTML
	DVB-Sub	Burn in

HLS Output Container

The following table lists supported output caption formats for this output container, sorted by the input caption container and input caption format.

Embedded captions formats include:

- CEA-608

- EIA-608

- CEA-708

- EIA-708

Ancillary captions include:

- Captions in the Quicktime Captions Track

- Captions in the MXF container VANC data

Note

For HLS outputs, if your input caption format is Teletext or DVB-Sub, you can include output captions in those formats as well. Standard Apple players will not recognize those captions, but custom players may.

Note

AWS Elemental MediaConvert has the following limitations with Teletext in outputs:
The service doesn't support captions formatting and positioning You can use only Teletext level 1.5 languages

Input Caption Container	Input Caption Format	Supported Output Caption Formats
MP4 Container	Embedded	Burn-inEmbeddedWeb-VTT
MXF Container	Embedded	Burn-inEmbeddedWeb-VTT
	Ancillary	Burn-inEmbeddedWeb-VTT
	Teletext	Burn inTTML
QuickTime Container	Embedded	Burn-inEmbeddedWeb-VTT
	Ancillary	Burn-inEmbeddedWeb-VTT
Raw Container	SRT	Burn-inWeb-VTT
	TTML	Burn-inWeb-VTT
	STL	Burn-inWeb-VTT
	SCC	Burn-inEmbeddedWeb-VTT
MPEG2-TS Container	Embedded	Burn-inEmbeddedWeb-VTT
	Teletext	Burn-inWeb-VTT
	DVB-Sub	Burn-in

MS Smooth (MSS) Output Container

The following table lists supported output caption formats for this output container, sorted by the input caption container and input caption format.

Embedded captions formats include:

- CEA-608

- EIA-608

- CEA-708

- EIA-708

Ancillary captions include:

- Captions in the Quicktime Captions Track

- Captions in the MXF container VANC data

Input Caption Container	Input Caption Format	Supported Output Caption Formats
MP4 Container	Embedded	Burn-inTTML
MXF Container	Embedded	Burn-inTTML

Input Caption Container	Input Caption Format	Supported Output Caption Formats
	Ancillary	Burn-inTTML
	Teletext	Burn-inTTML
QuickTime Container	Embedded	Burn-inTTML
	Ancillary	Burn-inTTML
Raw Container	SRT	Burn-inTTML
	SMI	Burn-inTTML
	TTML	Burn-inTTML
	STL	Burn-inTTML
	SCC	Burn-inTTML
MPEG2-TS Container	Embedded	Burn-inTTML
	Teletext	Burn-inTTML
	DVB-Sub	

MP4 Output Container

The following table lists supported output caption formats for this output container, sorted by the input caption container and input caption format.

Embedded captions formats include:

- CEA-608
- EIA-608
- CEA-708
- EIA-708

Ancillary captions include:

- Captions in the Quicktime Captions Track
- Captions in the MXF container VANC data

Input Caption Container	Input Caption Format	Supported Output Caption Formats
MP4 Container	Embedded	Burn InEmbedded
MXF Container	Embedded	Burn InEmbedded
	Ancillary	Burn InEmbedded
	Teletext	Burn InEmbedded
QuickTime Container	Embedded	Burn InEmbedded
	Ancillary	Burn InEmbedded
Raw Container	SRT	Burn In
	TTML	Burn In
	STL	Burn In
	SCC	Burn InEmbedded
MPEG2-TS Container	Embedded	Burn InEmbedded
	Teletext	Burn In
	DVB-Sub	Burn In

MPEG2-TS File Output Container

The following table lists supported output caption formats for this output container, sorted by the input caption container and input caption format.

Embedded captions formats include:

- CEA-608
- EIA-608
- CEA-708
- EIA-708

Ancillary captions include:

- Captions in the Quicktime Captions Track
- Captions in the MXF container VANC data

Note
AWS Elemental MediaConvert has the following limitations with Teletext in outputs:
The service doesn't support captions formatting and positioning You can use only Teletext level 1.5 languages

Input Caption Container	Input Caption Format	Supported Output Caption Formats
MP4 Container	Embedded	Burn-in DVB-Sub Embedded
MXF Container	Embedded	Burn-in DVB-Sub Embedded
	Ancillary	Burn-in DVB-Sub Embedded
	Teletext	Burn-in DVB-Sub Teletext
QuickTime Container	Embedded	Burn-in DVB-Sub Embedded
	Ancillary	Burn-in DVB-Sub Embedded
Raw Container	SRT	Burn-inTeletext
	SMI	Burn-inDVB-Sub
	TTML	Burn-inTeletextDVB-Sub
	STL	Burn-inTeletextDVB-Sub
	SCC	Burn-inDVB-SubEmbedded
MPEG2-TS Container	Embedded	Burn-inDVB-SubEmbedded
	Teletext	Burn-inDVB-SubTeletext
	DVB-Sub	Burn-inDVB-Sub

QuickTime Output Container

The following table lists supported output caption formats for this output container, sorted by the input caption container and input caption format.

Embedded captions formats include:

- CEA-608
- EIA-608
- CEA-708
- EIA-708

Ancillary captions include:

- Captions in the Quicktime Captions Track

- Captions in the MXF container VANC data

Input Caption Container	Input Caption Format	Supported Output Caption Formats
MP4 Container	Embedded	Burn-inEmbedded
MXF Container	Embedded	Burn-inEmbedded
	Ancillary	Burn-inEmbedded
	Teletext	Burn-in
QuickTime Container	Embedded	Burn-inEmbedded
	Ancillary	Burn-inEmbedded
Raw Container	SRT	Burn-in
	TTML	Burn-in
	STL	Burn-in
	SCC	Burn-inEmbedded
MPEG2-TS Container	Embedded	Burn-inEmbedded
	Teletext	Burn-in
	DVB-Sub	Burn-in

No Output Container

The following table lists supported output caption formats for this output container, sorted by the input caption container and input caption format.

Embedded captions formats include:

- CEA-608

- EIA-608

- CEA-708

- EIA-708

Ancillary captions include:

- Captions in the Quicktime Captions Track

- Captions in the MXF container VANC data

Input Caption Container	Input Caption Format	Supported Output Caption Formats
MP4 Container	Embedded	Burn-inEmbedded
MXF Container	Embedded	Burn-inEmbedded
	Ancillary	Burn-inEmbedded
	Teletext	Burn-in
QuickTime Container	Embedded	Burn-inEmbedded
	Ancillary	Burn-inEmbedded
Raw Container	SRT	Burn-in
	TTML	Burn-in
	STL	Burn-in
	SCC	Burn-inEmbedded
MPEG2-TS Container	Embedded	Burn-inEmbedded
	Teletext	Burn-in
	DVB-Sub	Burn-in

Example Job Settings

The provided job settings are recommended values that should work well for most jobs. Adapt them as necessary to suit your specific workflow.

To use these examples, replace the following placeholder values with actual values:

- ROLE HERE
- s3://INPUT HERE
- s3://OUTPUT HERE
- Example—mp4 Output
- Example—ABR Output

Example—mp4 Output

```
1  {
2    "UserMetadata": {},
3    "Role": "ROLE ARN",
4    "Settings": {
5      "OutputGroups": [
6        {
7          "Name": "File Group",
8          "OutputGroupSettings": {
9            "Type": "FILE_GROUP_SETTINGS",
10           "FileGroupSettings": {
11             "Destination": "s3://bucket/out"
12           }
13         },
14         "Outputs": [
15           {
16             "VideoDescription": {
17               "ScalingBehavior": "DEFAULT",
18               "TimecodeInsertion": "DISABLED",
19               "AntiAlias": "ENABLED",
20               "Sharpness": 50,
21               "CodecSettings": {
22                 "Codec": "H_264",
23                 "H264Settings": {
24                   "InterlaceMode": "PROGRESSIVE",
25                   "NumberReferenceFrames": 3,
26                   "Syntax": "DEFAULT",
27                   "Softness": 0,
28                   "GopClosedCadence": 1,
29                   "GopSize": 48,
30                   "Slices": 1,
31                   "GopBReference": "DISABLED",
32                   "SlowPal": "DISABLED",
33                   "SpatialAdaptiveQuantization": "ENABLED",
34                   "TemporalAdaptiveQuantization": "ENABLED",
35                   "FlickerAdaptiveQuantization": "DISABLED",
36                   "EntropyEncoding": "CABAC",
37                   "Bitrate": 4500000,
```

72

```
38        "FramerateControl": "SPECIFIED",
39        "RateControlMode": "CBR",
40        "CodecProfile": "HIGH",
41        "Telecine": "NONE",
42        "MinIInterval": 0,
43        "AdaptiveQuantization": "HIGH",
44        "CodecLevel": "LEVEL_4_1",
45        "FieldEncoding": "PAFF",
46        "SceneChangeDetect": "ENABLED",
47        "QualityTuningLevel": "SINGLE_PASS_HQ",
48        "FramerateConversionAlgorithm": "DUPLICATE_DROP",
49        "UnregisteredSeiTimecode": "DISABLED",
50        "GopSizeUnits": "FRAMES",
51        "ParControl": "INITIALIZE_FROM_SOURCE",
52        "NumberBFramesBetweenReferenceFrames": 3,
53        "RepeatPps": "DISABLED",
54        "HrdBufferSize": 9000000,
55        "HrdBufferInitialFillPercentage": 90,
56        "FramerateNumerator": 24000,
57        "FramerateDenominator": 1001
58      }
59    },
60    "AfdSignaling": "NONE",
61    "DropFrameTimecode": "ENABLED",
62    "RespondToAfd": "NONE",
63    "ColorMetadata": "INSERT",
64    "Width": 1920,
65    "Height": 1080
66  },
67  "AudioDescriptions": [
68    {
69      "AudioTypeControl": "FOLLOW_INPUT",
70      "CodecSettings": {
71        "Codec": "AAC",
72        "AacSettings": {
73          "AudioDescriptionBroadcasterMix": "NORMAL",
74          "Bitrate": 96000,
75          "RateControlMode": "CBR",
76          "CodecProfile": "LC",
77          "CodingMode": "CODING_MODE_2_0",
78          "RawFormat": "NONE",
79          "SampleRate": 48000,
80          "Specification": "MPEG4"
81        }
82      },
83      "LanguageCodeControl": "FOLLOW_INPUT"
84    }
85  ],
86  "ContainerSettings": {
87    "Container": "MP4",
88    "Mp4Settings": {
89      "CslgAtom": "INCLUDE",
90      "FreeSpaceBox": "EXCLUDE",
91      "MoovPlacement": "PROGRESSIVE_DOWNLOAD"
```

```
 92                     }
 93                   }
 94                 }
 95               ]
 96             }
 97           ],
 98           "AdAvailOffset": 0,
 99           "Inputs": [
100             {
101               "AudioSelectors": {
102                 "Audio Selector 1": {
103                   "Tracks": [
104                     1
105                   ],
106                   "Offset": 0,
107                   "DefaultSelection": "DEFAULT",
108                   "SelectorType": "TRACK",
109                   "ProgramSelection": 1
110                 },
111                 "Audio Selector 2": {
112                   "Tracks": [
113                     2
114                   ],
115                   "Offset": 0,
116                   "DefaultSelection": "NOT_DEFAULT",
117                   "SelectorType": "TRACK",
118                   "ProgramSelection": 1
119                 }
120               },
121               "VideoSelector": {
122                 "ColorSpace": "FOLLOW"
123               },
124               "FilterEnable": "AUTO",
125               "PsiControl": "USE_PSI",
126               "FilterStrength": 0,
127               "DeblockFilter": "DISABLED",
128               "DenoiseFilter": "DISABLED",
129               "TimecodeSource": "EMBEDDED",
130               "FileInput": "s3://input"
131             }
132           ]
133         }
134 }
```

Example—ABR Output

```
 1 {
 2   "UserMetadata": {},
 3   "Role": "ROLE ARN",
 4   "Settings": {
 5     "OutputGroups": [
 6       {
 7         "Name": "Apple HLS",
 8         "Outputs": [
```

```
 9        {
10            "ContainerSettings": {
11              "Container": "M3U8",
12              "M3u8Settings": {
13                "AudioFramesPerPes": 2,
14                "PcrControl": "PCR_EVERY_PES_PACKET",
15                "PmtPid": 480,
16                "PrivateMetadataPid": 503,
17                "ProgramNumber": 1,
18                "PatInterval": 100,
19                "PmtInterval": 100,
20                "VideoPid": 481,
21                "AudioPids": [
22                  482,
23                  483,
24                  484,
25                  485,
26                  486,
27                  487,
28                  488,
29                  489,
30                  490,
31                  491,
32                  492
33                ]
34              }
35            },
36            "VideoDescription": {
37              "Width": 1920,
38              "Height": 1080,
39              "VideoPreprocessors": {
40                "Deinterlacer": {
41                  "Algorithm": "INTERPOLATE",
42                  "Mode": "DEINTERLACE"
43                }
44              },
45              "AntiAlias": "ENABLED",
46              "Sharpness": 100,
47              "CodecSettings": {
48                "Codec": "H_264",
49                "H264Settings": {
50                  "InterlaceMode": "PROGRESSIVE",
51                  "ParNumerator": 1,
52                  "NumberReferenceFrames": 3,
53                  "Softness": 0,
54                  "FramerateDenominator": 1001,
55                  "GopClosedCadence": 1,
56                  "GopSize": 90,
57                  "Slices": 1,
58                  "HrdBufferSize": 12500000,
59                  "ParDenominator": 1,
60                  "SpatialAdaptiveQuantization": "ENABLED",
61                  "TemporalAdaptiveQuantization": "DISABLED",
62                  "FlickerAdaptiveQuantization": "DISABLED",
```

```
63              "EntropyEncoding": "CABAC",
64              "Bitrate": 8500000,
65              "FramerateControl": "SPECIFIED",
66              "RateControlMode": "CBR",
67              "CodecProfile": "HIGH",
68              "Telecine": "NONE",
69              "FramerateNumerator": 30000,
70              "MinIInterval": 0,
71              "AdaptiveQuantization": "MEDIUM",
72              "CodecLevel": "LEVEL_4",
73              "SceneChangeDetect": "ENABLED",
74              "QualityTuningLevel": "SINGLE_PASS_HQ",
75              "GopSizeUnits": "FRAMES",
76              "ParControl": "SPECIFIED",
77              "NumberBFramesBetweenReferenceFrames": 3,
78              "HrdBufferInitialFillPercentage": 90,
79              "Syntax": "DEFAULT"
80            }
81          },
82          "AfdSignaling": "NONE",
83          "DropFrameTimecode": "ENABLED",
84          "RespondToAfd": "NONE",
85          "ColorMetadata": "INSERT"
86        },
87        "AudioDescriptions": [
88          {
89            "AudioTypeControl": "FOLLOW_INPUT",
90            "AudioSourceName": "Audio Selector 1",
91            "CodecSettings": {
92              "Codec": "AAC",
93              "AacSettings": {
94                "Bitrate": 128000,
95                "RateControlMode": "CBR",
96                "CodecProfile": "LC",
97                "CodingMode": "CODING_MODE_2_0",
98                "SampleRate": 48000
99              }
100           },
101           "LanguageCodeControl": "FOLLOW_INPUT"
102         }
103       ],
104       "NameModifier": "_high"
105     },
106     {
107       "VideoDescription": {
108         "ScalingBehavior": "DEFAULT",
109         "TimecodeInsertion": "DISABLED",
110         "AntiAlias": "ENABLED",
111         "Sharpness": 50,
112         "CodecSettings": {
113           "Codec": "H_264",
114           "H264Settings": {
115             "InterlaceMode": "PROGRESSIVE",
116             "NumberReferenceFrames": 3,
```

```
117          "Syntax": "DEFAULT",
118          "Softness": 0,
119          "GopClosedCadence": 1,
120          "GopSize": 90,
121          "Slices": 1,
122          "GopBReference": "DISABLED",
123          "SlowPal": "DISABLED",
124          "SpatialAdaptiveQuantization": "ENABLED",
125          "TemporalAdaptiveQuantization": "ENABLED",
126          "FlickerAdaptiveQuantization": "DISABLED",
127          "EntropyEncoding": "CABAC",
128          "Bitrate": 7500000,
129          "FramerateControl": "INITIALIZE_FROM_SOURCE",
130          "RateControlMode": "CBR",
131          "CodecProfile": "MAIN",
132          "Telecine": "NONE",
133          "MinIInterval": 0,
134          "AdaptiveQuantization": "HIGH",
135          "CodecLevel": "AUTO",
136          "FieldEncoding": "PAFF",
137          "SceneChangeDetect": "ENABLED",
138          "QualityTuningLevel": "SINGLE_PASS",
139          "FramerateConversionAlgorithm": "DUPLICATE_DROP",
140          "UnregisteredSeiTimecode": "DISABLED",
141          "GopSizeUnits": "FRAMES",
142          "ParControl": "INITIALIZE_FROM_SOURCE",
143          "NumberBFramesBetweenReferenceFrames": 2,
144          "RepeatPps": "DISABLED"
145        }
146      },
147      "AfdSignaling": "NONE",
148      "DropFrameTimecode": "ENABLED",
149      "RespondToAfd": "NONE",
150      "ColorMetadata": "INSERT",
151      "Width": 1280,
152      "Height": 720
153    },
154    "AudioDescriptions": [
155      {
156        "AudioTypeControl": "FOLLOW_INPUT",
157        "CodecSettings": {
158          "Codec": "AAC",
159          "AacSettings": {
160            "AudioDescriptionBroadcasterMix": "NORMAL",
161            "Bitrate": 96000,
162            "RateControlMode": "CBR",
163            "CodecProfile": "LC",
164            "CodingMode": "CODING_MODE_2_0",
165            "RawFormat": "NONE",
166            "SampleRate": 48000,
167            "Specification": "MPEG4"
168          }
169        },
170        "LanguageCodeControl": "FOLLOW_INPUT"
```

```
171                   }
172                 ],
173               "OutputSettings": {
174                 "HlsSettings": {
175                   "AudioGroupId": "program_audio",
176                   "AudioRenditionSets": "program_audio",
177                   "IFrameOnlyManifest": "EXCLUDE"
178                 }
179               },
180               "ContainerSettings": {
181                 "Container": "M3U8",
182                 "M3u8Settings": {
183                   "AudioFramesPerPes": 4,
184                   "PcrControl": "PCR_EVERY_PES_PACKET",
185                   "PmtPid": 480,
186                   "PrivateMetadataPid": 503,
187                   "ProgramNumber": 1,
188                   "PatInterval": 0,
189                   "PmtInterval": 0,
190                   "Scte35Source": "NONE",
191                   "Scte35Pid": 500,
192                   "TimedMetadata": "NONE",
193                   "TimedMetadataPid": 502,
194                   "VideoPid": 481,
195                   "AudioPids": [
196                     482,
197                     483,
198                     484,
199                     485,
200                     486,
201                     487,
202                     488,
203                     489,
204                     490,
205                     491,
206                     492
207                   ]
208                 }
209               },
210               "NameModifier": "_med"
211             },
212             {
213               "VideoDescription": {
214                 "ScalingBehavior": "DEFAULT",
215                 "TimecodeInsertion": "DISABLED",
216                 "AntiAlias": "ENABLED",
217                 "Sharpness": 100,
218                 "CodecSettings": {
219                   "Codec": "H_264",
220                   "H264Settings": {
221                     "InterlaceMode": "PROGRESSIVE",
222                     "NumberReferenceFrames": 3,
223                     "Syntax": "DEFAULT",
224                     "Softness": 0,
```

```
225          "GopClosedCadence": 1,
226          "GopSize": 90,
227          "Slices": 1,
228          "GopBReference": "DISABLED",
229          "SlowPal": "DISABLED",
230          "SpatialAdaptiveQuantization": "ENABLED",
231          "TemporalAdaptiveQuantization": "ENABLED",
232          "FlickerAdaptiveQuantization": "DISABLED",
233          "EntropyEncoding": "CABAC",
234          "Bitrate": 3500000,
235          "FramerateControl": "INITIALIZE_FROM_SOURCE",
236          "RateControlMode": "CBR",
237          "CodecProfile": "MAIN",
238          "Telecine": "NONE",
239          "MinIInterval": 0,
240          "AdaptiveQuantization": "HIGH",
241          "CodecLevel": "LEVEL_3_1",
242          "FieldEncoding": "PAFF",
243          "SceneChangeDetect": "ENABLED",
244          "QualityTuningLevel": "SINGLE_PASS_HQ",
245          "FramerateConversionAlgorithm": "DUPLICATE_DROP",
246          "UnregisteredSeiTimecode": "DISABLED",
247          "GopSizeUnits": "FRAMES",
248          "ParControl": "INITIALIZE_FROM_SOURCE",
249          "NumberBFramesBetweenReferenceFrames": 2,
250          "RepeatPps": "DISABLED"
251        }
252      },
253      "AfdSignaling": "NONE",
254      "DropFrameTimecode": "ENABLED",
255      "RespondToAfd": "NONE",
256      "ColorMetadata": "INSERT",
257      "Width": 960,
258      "Height": 540
259    },
260    "AudioDescriptions": [
261      {
262        "AudioTypeControl": "FOLLOW_INPUT",
263        "CodecSettings": {
264          "Codec": "AAC",
265          "AacSettings": {
266            "AudioDescriptionBroadcasterMix": "NORMAL",
267            "Bitrate": 96000,
268            "RateControlMode": "CBR",
269            "CodecProfile": "LC",
270            "CodingMode": "CODING_MODE_2_0",
271            "RawFormat": "NONE",
272            "SampleRate": 48000,
273            "Specification": "MPEG4"
274          }
275        },
276        "LanguageCodeControl": "FOLLOW_INPUT"
277      }
278    ],
```

```
279          "OutputSettings": {
280            "HlsSettings": {
281              "AudioGroupId": "program_audio",
282              "AudioRenditionSets": "program_audio",
283              "IFrameOnlyManifest": "EXCLUDE"
284            }
285          },
286          "ContainerSettings": {
287            "Container": "M3U8",
288            "M3u8Settings": {
289              "AudioFramesPerPes": 4,
290              "PcrControl": "PCR_EVERY_PES_PACKET",
291              "PmtPid": 480,
292              "PrivateMetadataPid": 503,
293              "ProgramNumber": 1,
294              "PatInterval": 0,
295              "PmtInterval": 0,
296              "Scte35Source": "NONE",
297              "Scte35Pid": 500,
298              "TimedMetadata": "NONE",
299              "TimedMetadataPid": 502,
300              "VideoPid": 481,
301              "AudioPids": [
302                482,
303                483,
304                484,
305                485,
306                486,
307                487,
308                488,
309                489,
310                490,
311                491,
312                492
313              ]
314            }
315          },
316          "NameModifier": "_low"
317        }
318      ],
319      "OutputGroupSettings": {
320        "Type": "HLS_GROUP_SETTINGS",
321        "HlsGroupSettings": {
322          "ManifestDurationFormat": "INTEGER",
323          "SegmentLength": 10,
324          "TimedMetadataId3Period": 10,
325          "CaptionLanguageSetting": "OMIT",
326          "Destination": "s3://bucket/hls1/master",
327          "TimedMetadataId3Frame": "PRIV",
328          "CodecSpecification": "RFC_4281",
329          "OutputSelection": "MANIFESTS_AND_SEGMENTS",
330          "ProgramDateTimePeriod": 600,
331          "MinSegmentLength": 0,
332          "DirectoryStructure": "SINGLE_DIRECTORY",
```

```
333          "ProgramDateTime": "EXCLUDE",
334          "SegmentControl": "SEGMENTED_FILES",
335          "ManifestCompression": "NONE",
336          "ClientCache": "ENABLED",
337          "StreamInfResolution": "INCLUDE"
338        }
339      }
340    }
341  ],
342  "AdAvailOffset": 0,
343  "Inputs": [
344    {
345      "AudioSelectors": {
346        "Audio Selector 1": {
347          "Tracks": [
348            1
349          ],
350          "Offset": 0,
351          "DefaultSelection": "DEFAULT",
352          "SelectorType": "TRACK",
353          "ProgramSelection": 1
354        },
355        "Audio Selector 2": {
356          "Tracks": [
357            2
358          ],
359          "Offset": 0,
360          "DefaultSelection": "NOT_DEFAULT",
361          "SelectorType": "TRACK",
362          "ProgramSelection": 1
363        }
364      },
365      "VideoSelector": {
366        "ColorSpace": "FOLLOW"
367      },
368      "FilterEnable": "AUTO",
369      "PsiControl": "USE_PSI",
370      "FilterStrength": 0,
371      "DeblockFilter": "DISABLED",
372      "DenoiseFilter": "DISABLED",
373      "TimecodeSource": "EMBEDDED",
374      "FileInput": "s3://INPUT"
375    }
376  ]
377  }
378 }
```

Postman Collection Files

Import these collection files into Postman to access AWS Elemental MediaConvert via the REST API.

- GET Collection
- POST Collection

GET Collection

```
1  {
2      "owner": "2332976",
3      "lastUpdatedBy": "2332976",
4      "lastRevision": 1921667904,
5      "team": null,
6      "id": "87fac2df-dd0f-b54a-b1f9-5b138cb4147f",
7      "name": "EMF Get",
8      "description": "EMF Get Template",
9      "folders_order": [],
10     "order": [
11         "bc671df5-4a85-54b6-f137-19cb70516fd2",
12         "85318a0b-c490-3718-62eb-2a737de83af0",
13         "1fd40def-ca4b-1842-c99a-778f62269010"
14     ],
15     "folders": [],
16     "hasRequests": true,
17     "requests": [
18         {
19             "id": "1fd40def-ca4b-1842-c99a-778f62269010",
20             "headers": "Content-Type: application/json\n",
21             "headerData": [
22                 {
23                     "key": "Content-Type",
24                     "value": "application/json",
25                     "description": "",
26                     "enabled": true
27                 }
28             ],
29             "url": "https://<custom-account-id>.mediaconvert.<region>.amazonaws.com/2017-08-29/
                    queues",
30             "folder": null,
31             "queryParams": [],
32             "preRequestScript": null,
33             "pathVariables": {},
34             "pathVariableData": [],
35             "method": "GET",
36             "data": null,
37             "dataMode": "params",
38             "tests": null,
39             "currentHelper": "awsSigV4",
40             "helperAttributes": {
41                 "accessKey": "AccessKey",
42                 "secretKey": "ScretKey",
43                 "region": "supported-region",
44                 "service": "mediaconvert",
45                 "saveToRequest": true
46             },
47             "time": 1513791262493,
48             "name": "GET List Queue ",
49             "description": "",
50             "collectionId": "87fac2df-dd0f-b54a-b1f9-5b138cb4147f",
51             "responses": []
```

```
52          },
53          {
54              "id": "85318a0b-c490-3718-62eb-2a737de83af0",
55              "headers": "Content-Type: application/json\n",
56              "headerData": [
57                  {
58                      "key": "Content-Type",
59                      "value": "application/json",
60                      "description": "",
61                      "enabled": true
62                  }
63              ],
64              "url": "https://<custom-account-id>.mediaconvert.<region>.amazonaws.com/2017-08-29/
                      queues/<QUEUE-NAME-HERE>",
65              "folder": null,
66              "queryParams": [],
67              "preRequestScript": null,
68              "pathVariables": {},
69              "pathVariableData": [],
70              "method": "GET",
71              "data": null,
72              "dataMode": "params",
73              "tests": null,
74              "currentHelper": "awsSigV4",
75              "helperAttributes": {
76                  "accessKey": "AccessKey",
77                  "secretKey": "SecretKey",
78                  "region": "supported-region",
79                  "service": "mediaconvert",
80                  "saveToRequest": true
81              },
82              "time": 1507243078514,
83              "name": "GET Queue Details",
84              "description": "",
85              "collectionId": "87fac2df-dd0f-b54a-b1f9-5b138cb4147f",
86              "responses": []
87          },
88          {
89              "id": "bc671df5-4a85-54b6-f137-19cb70516fd2",
90              "headers": "Content-Type: application/json\n",
91              "headerData": [
92                  {
93                      "key": "Content-Type",
94                      "value": "application/json",
95                      "description": "",
96                      "enabled": true
97                  }
98              ],
99              "url": "https://<custom-account-id>.mediaconvert.<region>.amazonaws.com/2017-08-29/
                      jobs/<job-id>",
100             "folder": null,
101             "queryParams": [],
102             "preRequestScript": null,
103             "pathVariables": {},
```
83

```
104        "pathVariableData": [],
105        "method": "GET",
106        "data": null,
107        "dataMode": "params",
108        "tests": null,
109        "currentHelper": "awsSigV4",
110        "helperAttributes": {
111            "accessKey": "AccessKey",
112            "secretKey": "SecretKey",
113            "region": "supportedregion",
114            "service": "mediaconvert",
115            "saveToRequest": true
116        },
117        "time": 1510272337434,
118        "name": "GET JOB ID",
119        "description": "",
120        "collectionId": "87fac2df-dd0f-b54a-b1f9-5b138cb4147f",
121        "responses": []
122    }
123    ]
124 }
```

POST Collection

```
1  {
2      "id": "a1be92f5-37d5-aaf0-06bb-14090d825c62",
3      "name": "AWS Elemental MediaConvert POST",
4      "description": "POST Template",
5      "order": [
6          "0fd3c4a5-fa08-2dbc-1f0a-955942664858",
7          "d6ffaf05-0caa-35ee-8a3d-4457a96f4926"
8      ],
9      "folders": [],
10     "folders_order": [],
11     "timestamp": 0,
12     "owner": "2332976",
13     "public": false,
14     "requests": [
15         {
16             "id": "0fd3c4a5-fa08-2dbc-1f0a-955942664858",
17             "headers": "Content-Type: application/json\n",
18             "headerData": [
19                 {
20                     "key": "Content-Type",
21                     "value": "application/json",
22                     "description": "",
23                     "enabled": true
24                 }
25             ],
26             "url": "https://<custom-account-id>.mediaconvert.<region>.amazonaws.com
                   /2017-08-29/",
27             "folder": null,
28             "queryParams": [
29                 {
```

```
30          "key": "AWS_Region",
31          "value": "eu-west-1",
32          "equals": false,
33          "description": "",
34          "enabled": false
35        },
36        {
37          "key": "AWS_Access_Key",
38          "value": "KEY",
39          "equals": false,
40          "description": "",
41          "enabled": false
42        },
43        {
44          "key": "AWS_Secret_Key",
45          "value": "KEY",
46          "equals": false,
47          "description": "",
48          "enabled": false
49        }
50      ],
51      "preRequestScript": "",
52      "pathVariables": {},
53      "pathVariableData": [],
54      "method": "POST",
55      "data": [],
56      "dataMode": "raw",
57      "tests": "",
58      "currentHelper": "awsSigV4",
59      "helperAttributes": {
60        "accessKey": "AccessKey",
61        "secretKey": "SecretKey",
62        "region": "supported-region",
63        "service": "mediaconvert",
64        "saveToRequest": true
65      },
66      "time": 1510272274641,
67      "name": "Post MP4 Job",
68      "description": "",
69      "collectionId": "a1be92f5-37d5-aaf0-06bb-14090d825c62",
70      "responses": [],
71      "rawModeData": "{\r\n  \"userMetadata\": {},\r\n  \"role\": \"ROLE ARN HERE\",\r\n
          \"settings\": {\r\n    \"outputGroups\": [\r\n      {\r\n        \"name\": \"
          File Group\",\r\n        \"outputs\": [\r\n          {\r\n            \"
          containerSettings\": {\r\n              \"container\": \"MP4\",\r\n
                \"mp4Settings\": {\r\n                \"cslgAtom\": \"INCLUDE\",\r\
          n                \"freeSpaceBox\": \"EXCLUDE\",\r\n                \"
          moovPlacement\": \"PROGRESSIVE_DOWNLOAD\"\r\n              }\r\n            },\r
          \n            \"videoDescription\": {\r\n              \"scalingBehavior\": \"
          DEFAULT\",\r\n              \"timecodeInsertion\": \"DISABLED\",\r\n
                \"antiAlias\": \"ENABLED\",\r\n              \"sharpness\": 50,\r\n
                \"codecSettings\": {\r\n                \"codec\": \"H_264\",\r\n
                \"h264Settings\": {\r\n                  \"interlaceMode\": \"
          PROGRESSIVE\",\r\n                  \"numberReferenceFrames\": 1,\r\n
```

\"syntax\": \"DEFAULT\",\r\n   \"softness\": 0,\r\n   \"gopClosedCadence\": 1,\r\n   \"gopSize\": 90,\r\n   \"slices\": 1,\r\n   \"gopBReference\": \"DISABLED\",\r\n   \"slowPal\": \"DISABLED\",\r\n   \"spatialAdaptiveQuantization\": \"ENABLED\",\r\n   \"temporalAdaptiveQuantization\": \"ENABLED\",\r\n   \"flickerAdaptiveQuantization\": \"ENABLED\",\r\n   \"entropyEncoding\": \"CABAC\",\r\n   \"bitrate\": 5000000,\r\n   \"framerateControl\": \"INITIALIZE_FROM_SOURCE\",\r\n   \"rateControlMode\": \"CBR\",\r\n   \"codecProfile\": \"MAIN\",\r\n   \"telecine\": \"NONE\",\r\n   \"minIInterval\": 0,\r\n   \"adaptiveQuantization\": \"MEDIUM\",\r\n   \"codecLevel\": \"AUTO\",\r\n   \"fieldEncoding\": \"PAFF\",\r\n   \"sceneChangeDetect\": \"ENABLED\",\r\n   \"qualityTuningLevel\": \"SINGLE_PASS\",\r\n   \"framerateConversionAlgorithm\": \"DUPLICATE_DROP\",\r\n   \"unregisteredSeiTimecode\": \"DISABLED\",\r\n   \"gopSizeUnits\": \"FRAMES\",\r\n   \"parControl\": \"INITIALIZE_FROM_SOURCE\",\r\n   \"numberBFramesBetweenReferenceFrames\": 2,\r\n   \"repeatPps\": \"DISABLED\"\r\n   }\r\n   },\r\n   \"afdSignaling\": \"NONE\",\r\n   \"dropFrameTimecode\": \"ENABLED\",\r\n   \"respondToAfd\": \"NONE\",\r\n   \"colorMetadata\": \"INSERT\"\r\n   },\r\n   \"audioDescriptions\": [\r\n   {\r\n   \"audioTypeControl\": \"FOLLOW_INPUT\",\r\n   \"codecSettings\": {\r\n   \"codec\": \"AAC\",\r\n   \"aacSettings\": {\r\n   \"audioDescriptionBroadcasterMix\": \"NORMAL\",\r\n   \"bitrate\": 96000,\r\n   \"rateControlMode\": \"CBR\",\r\n   \"codecProfile\": \"LC\",\r\n   \"codingMode\": \"CODING_MODE_2_0\",\r\n   \"rawFormat\": \"NONE\",\r\n   \"sampleRate\": 48000,\r\n   \"specification\": \"MPEG4\"\r\n   }\r\n   },\r\n   \"languageCodeControl\": \"FOLLOW_INPUT\"\r\n   }\r\n   ]\r\n   }\r\n   ],   \"outputGroupSettings\": {\r\n   \"type\": \"FILE_GROUP_SETTINGS\",\r\n   \"fileGroupSettings\": {\r\n   \"destination\": \"s3://test/test\"\r\n   }\r\n   }\r\n   }\r\n   ],   \"adAvailOffset\": 0,   \"inputs\": [\r\n   {\r\n n   \"audioSelectors\": {\r\n   \"Audio Selector 1\": {\r\n   \"offset\": 0,\r\n   \"defaultSelection\": \"DEFAULT\",\r\n   \"programSelection\": 1\r\n   }\r\n   },   \"videoSelector\": {\r\n   \"colorSpace\": \"FOLLOW\"\r\n   },\r\n   \"filterEnable\": \"AUTO\",\r\n   \"psiControl\": \"USE_PSI\",\r\n   \"filterStrength\": 0,\r\n   \"deblockFilter\": \"DISABLED\",\r\n   \"denoiseFilter\": \"DISABLED\",\r\n   \"timecodeSource\": \"EMBEDDED\",\r\n   \"fileInput\": \"s3://bucket/file.mp4\"\r\n   }\r\n   ]\r\n }\r\n}"
    72   },
    73   {
    74   "id": "d6ffaf05-0caa-35ee-8a3d-4457a96f4926",
    75   "headers": "Content-Type: application/json\n",
    76   "headerData": [
    77   {
    78   "key": "Content-Type",

```
79              "value": "application/json",
80              "description": "",
81              "enabled": true
82          }
83      ],
84      "url": "https://mediaconvert.<region>.amazonaws.com/2017-08-29/endpoints",
85      "folder": null,
86      "queryParams": [
87          {
88              "key": "AWS_Region",
89              "value": "eu-west-1",
90              "equals": false,
91              "description": "",
92              "enabled": false
93          },
94          {
95              "key": "AWS_Access_Key",
96              "value": "KEY",
97              "equals": false,
98              "description": "",
99              "enabled": false
100         },
101         {
102             "key": "AWS_Secret_Key",
103             "value": "KEY",
104             "equals": false,
105             "description": "",
106             "enabled": false
107         }
108     ],
109     "preRequestScript": "",
110     "pathVariables": {},
111     "pathVariableData": [],
112     "method": "POST",
113     "data": [],
114     "dataMode": "raw",
115     "tests": "",
116     "currentHelper": "awsSigV4",
117     "helperAttributes": {
118         "accessKey": "AccessKey",
119         "secretKey": "SecretKey",
120         "region": "Supported Region",
121         "service": "mediaconvert",
122         "saveToRequest": true
123     },
124     "time": 1510272153358,
125     "name": "POST Request Account Endpoint",
126     "description": "",
127     "collectionId": "a1be92f5-37d5-aaf0-06bb-14090d825c62",
128     "responses": [],
129     "rawModeData": ""
130     }
131   ]
132 }
```

Monitoring AWS Elemental MediaConvert Jobs

You can keep on top of your AWS Elemental MediaConvert jobs in these ways:

- The *AWS Elemental MediaConvert Recent Jobs* page shows the status of your jobs. Access it by opening the AWS Elemental MediaConvert console and choosing **Jobs** in the navigation pane. You might need to choose the menu icon (the three-bar icon) in the upper-left corner of the console to open this navigation pane.

- *Amazon CloudWatch* monitors your AWS resources and the applications that you run on AWS in real-time. You can collect and track metrics, create customized dashboards, and set alarms that notify you or that take actions when a specified metric reaches a threshold that you specify. For example, you can have CloudWatch track the number of successful jobs over a specified period of time. For more information, see the Amazon CloudWatch User Guide. For a list of the AWS Elemental MediaConvert metrics that CloudWatch tracks, see [ERROR] BAD/MISSING LINK TEXT.

- *Amazon CloudWatch Events* delivers a near real-time stream of system events that describe changes in AWS resources. You can use CloudWatch Events to set up notifications for your job status changes. For more information and a tutorial on setting up job notifications, see [ERROR] BAD/MISSING LINK TEXT.

  You can also use CloudWatch Events to trigger automated actions in other AWS services when these events happen. A common use case for CloudWatch Events with AWS Elemental MediaConvert is to trigger a Lambda function to initiate your postprocessing. For more information, see the Amazon CloudWatch Events User Guide.

- *AWS CloudTrail* captures API calls and related events made by or on behalf of your AWS account and delivers the log files to an Amazon S3 bucket that you specify. You can identify which users and accounts called AWS, the source IP address from which the calls were made, and when the calls occurred. For more information, see .

CloudWatch Metrics

AWS Elemental MediaConvert sends the following metrics to CloudWatch every time the status of a job changes.

Metric	Description
HDOutputSeconds	The number of billable seconds of HD output for a queue. Valid Dimensions: Queue Unit: Seconds
SDOutputSeconds	The number of billable seconds of SD output for a queue. Valid Dimensions: Queue Unit: Seconds
UHDOutputSeconds	The number of billable seconds of UHD output for a queue. Valid Dimensions: Queue Unit: Seconds
AudioOutputSeconds	The number of billable seconds of audio output for a queue. Valid Dimensions: Queue Unit: Seconds
JobsCompletedCount	The number of jobs completed in this queue. Valid Dimensions: Queue Unit: Count
JobsErroredCount	The number of jobs that failed because of invalid inputs, such as a request to transcode a file that is not in the specified input bucket. Valid Dimensions: Queue Unit: Count
StandbyTime	The number of seconds before AWS Elemental MediaConvert starts transcoding a job. Valid Dimensions: Queue Unit: Seconds
TranscodingTime	The number of seconds for AWS Elemental MediaConvert to complete transcoding. Valid Dimensions: Queue Unit: Seconds
Errors	The number of errors caused by invalid operation parameters, such as a request for a job status that does not include the job ID. Valid Dimensions: Operation Unit: Count

Dimensions for AWS Elemental MediaConvert Metrics

AWS Elemental MediaConvert metrics use the `MediaConvert` namespace and provide metrics for the following dimensions.

Dimension	Description
Queue	CloudWatch shows information for the specified queue.
Job	CloudWatch shows information only for a single job.
Operation	CloudWatch shows information only for a single operation parameter, such as a job ID.

Working with CloudWatch Events and AWS Elemental MediaConvert

You can use Amazon CloudWatch Events to notify you when your job status changes and to trigger automated actions in other AWS services when these events happen. For example, you can set up CloudWatch Events to notify you if your AWS Elemental MediaConvert job fails. You can also set up CloudWatch Events so that a Lambda function initiates your post-processing code after your job finishes.

To set up CloudWatch Events, you create a rule that links AWS Elemental MediaConvert and the service that responds to your job status change, such as Amazon Simple Notification Service (SNS) or AWS Lambda. The following illustration shows these two parts of CloudWatch Events rules.

For example, you can create a rule and name it "MediaConvert Job Error". Next, you can set up an Amazon SNS topic that has the email address that you want the notification sent to. The event source is the event that AWS Elemental MediaConvert sends to CloudWatch when the status of a job changes to ERROR. For a tutorial on setting up this CloudWatch Events event rule, see [ERROR] BAD/MISSING LINK TEXT.

For more information about the events that AWS Elemental MediaConvert can send in the CloudWatch Events event stream, see [ERROR] BAD/MISSING LINK TEXT.

Tutorial: Setting Up Email Notifications for Failed Jobs

In this tutorial, you configure a CloudWatch Events event rule that captures events when a job status changes to ERROR and then notifies you about the event. To do this, you first create a topic in Amazon SNS that will send you an email notification about the failed job. Next, you create a rule in CloudWatch Events by defining an event source and referencing the Amazon SNS topic (the "target"), as shown in the following illustration.

- Prerequisites
- Step 1: Create a Topic in Amazon SNS
- Step 2: Specify an Event Source in a CloudWatch Events Rule
- Step 3: Add the Amazon SNS Topic and Finish Your Rule
- Step 4: Test Your Rule

Prerequisites

This tutorial assumes that you already know how to create AWS Elemental MediaConvert transcoding jobs. For information about creating jobs, see [ERROR] BAD/MISSING LINK TEXT. At the end of this tutorial, you can submit a job that you designed to fail, to test that you configured your Amazon SNS email notifications correctly.

Step 1: Create a Topic in Amazon SNS

The first part of setting up a CloudWatch Events rule is preparing the rule target. In this case, that means creating and subscribing to an Amazon SNS topic.

Amazon CloudWatch Events

Rule "Send me an email when one of my jobs has an error."

Target, Amazon SNS Topic "Use my SNS topic that sends an email to the address I provide."

Event Source "AWS Elemental MediaConvert says one of my jobs has an error."

To create an Amazon SNS topic

1. Open the Amazon SNS console at https://console.aws.amazon.com/sns/v2/home.

2. In the navigation pane, choose **Topics**, and then choose **Create new topic**.

3. For **Topic name**, type **MediaConvertJobErrorAlert**, and then choose **Create topic**.

4. Choose the topic ARN link for the topic that you just created. It looks something like this: **arn:aws:sns:region:123456789012:MediaConvertJobErrorAlert**.

5. On the **Topic details: MediaConvertJobErrorAlert** page, in the **Subscriptions** section, choose **Create subscription**.

6. For **Protocol**, choose **Email**. For **Endpoint**, enter the email address that you want Amazon SNS to send the notification to.

7. Choose **Create subscription**.

8. You will receive an email from AWS Notifications. When you receive it, choose the **Confirm subscription** link in the email.

Step 2: Specify an Event Source in a CloudWatch Events Rule

Next, specify your event source in a CloudWatch Events rule to capture only events that are generated by a job status that changes to ERROR.

To set up an event source in a CloudWatch Events rule

1. Open the CloudWatch console at https://console.aws.amazon.com/cloudwatch/.

2. In the navigation pane, choose **Events**, and then choose **Create rule**.

3. In the **Event Source** section, for **Build event pattern to match events by service**, choose **Custom event pattern**.

4. In the **Build custom event pattern** box, replace the existing text with the following text:

```
1  {
2  "source": [
3  "aws.mediaconvert"
4  ],
5  "detail": {
6  "status": [
7  "ERROR"
8  ]
9  }
10 }
```

This code defines a CloudWatch Events event rule that matches any event where the job status changes to `ERROR`. For more information about event patterns, see Events and Event Patterns in the *Amazon CloudWatch User Guide*.

Step 3: Add the Amazon SNS Topic and Finish Your Rule

Next, add the target (the Amazon SNS topic) that you created in Step 1 to the CloudWatch Events rule that you started in Step 2.

To add the SNS topic and finish the CloudWatch Events rule

1. In the **Targets** section, choose **Add targets**, and then change the default **Lambda function** to **SNS topic**.

2. For **Topic***, choose **MediaConvertJobErrorAlert**.

3. Choose the **Configure details** button.

4. For **Rule definition**, type a name and description for your rule, and then choose **Create rule**.

Step 4: Test Your Rule

To test your rule, submit a job that you know will cause an error. For example, specify an input location that does not exist. If you configured your event rule correctly, you should receive an email with the event text message in a few minutes.

To test the rule

1. Open the AWS Elemental MediaConvert console at https://console.aws.amazon.com/mediaconvert.

2. Submit a new AWS Elemental MediaConvert job. For more information, see [ERROR] BAD/MISSING LINK TEXT.

3. Check the email account that you specified when you set up your Amazon SNS topic. Confirm that you received an email notification for the job error.

AWS Elemental MediaConvert Events

AWS Elemental MediaConvert sends change events about the status of jobs to CloudWatch Events. You can create CloudWatch Events rules for any of the following events.

Job Status Change Events

Event	Sent When	Contains
PROGRESSING	A job moves from the SUBMITTED state to the PROGRESSING state.	Time in queue.
STATUS_UPDATE	Approximately one minute has elapsed since AWS Elemental MediaConvert began processing the job. Sent approximately every minute after that, until the service completes the transcode or encounters an error.	Job progress expressed in the number of frames transcoded since the beginning of the job.
COMPLETE	A job completes successfully. AWS Elemental MediaConvert generated all outputs without errors.	Warnings and output information about the completed job.
ERROR	A job has an error. At least one output has an error.	The error code or codes and any messages, as well as warnings or any other ephemeral job information about the job's error status.
INPUT_INFORMATION	Soon after AWS Elemental MediaConvert begins processing the job.	Media information, such as frame height and width, framerate, and codec. AWS Elemental MediaConvert includes information for all inputs in a single event.

95

Logging AWS Elemental MediaConvert API Calls with AWS Cloud-Trail

AWS Elemental MediaConvert is integrated with AWS CloudTrail, a service that provides a record of actions taken by a user, role, or an AWS service in AWS Elemental MediaConvert. If you create a trail, you can enable continuous delivery of CloudTrail events to an Amazon S3 bucket, Amazon CloudWatch Logs, and Amazon CloudWatch Events. AWS Elemental MediaConvert is also integrated with the **Event history** feature in CloudTrail. If an API for AWS Elemental MediaConvert is supported in **Event history**, you can view the most recent seven days of events in AWS Elemental MediaConvert in the CloudTrail console in **Event history** even if you have not configured any logs in CloudTrail. Using the information collected by CloudTrail, you can determine the request that was made to AWS Elemental MediaConvert, the IP address from which the request was made, who made the request, when it was made, and additional details.

To learn more about CloudTrail, including how to configure and enable it, see the AWS CloudTrail User Guide.

AWS Elemental MediaConvert Information in CloudTrail

CloudTrail is enabled on your AWS account when you create the account. When activity occurs in AWS Elemental MediaConvert, that activity is recorded in a CloudTrail event along with other AWS service events in **Event history**. You can view, search, and download the past seven days of supported activity in your AWS account. For more information, see Viewing Events with CloudTrail Event History and Services Supported by CloudTrail Event History.

All AWS Elemental MediaConvert actions are logged by CloudTrail and are documented in the AWS Elemental MediaConvert API Reference. For example, calls to the `CreateJob`, `ListPresets` and `DeleteQueue` sections generate entries in the CloudTrail log files.

Every event or log entry contains information about who generated the request. The identity information helps you determine the following:

- Whether the request was made with root or IAM user credentials.
- Whether the request was made with temporary security credentials for a role or federated user.
- Whether the request was made by another AWS service.

For more information, see the CloudTrail userIdentity Element.

You can view, search, and download the most recent seven days of AWS Elemental MediaConvert activity in the CloudTrail console. For more information, see Viewing Events with CloudTrail Event History. You can also create a trail and store your log files in your Amazon S3 bucket for as long as you want, and define Amazon S3 lifecycle rules to archive or delete log files automatically. By default, your log files are encrypted with Amazon S3 server-side encryption (SSE).

To be notified of log file delivery, configure CloudTrail to publish Amazon SNS notifications when new log files are delivered. For more information, see Configuring Amazon SNS Notifications for CloudTrail.

You can also aggregate AWS Elemental MediaConvert log files from multiple AWS regions and multiple AWS accounts into a single Amazon S3 bucket.

For more information, see Receiving CloudTrail Log Files from Multiple Regions and Receiving CloudTrail Log Files from Multiple Accounts.

Understanding AWS Elemental MediaConvert Log File Entries

A trail is a configuration that enables delivery of events as log files to an Amazon S3 bucket that you specify. CloudTrail log files contain one or more log entries. An event represents a single request from any source and includes information about the requested action, the date and time of the action, request parameters, and so on. CloudTrail log files are not an ordered stack trace of the public API calls, so they do not appear in any specific order.

The following example shows a CloudTrail log entry that demonstrates the CreateJob action.

```
1       {
2       "eventVersion":"1.05",
3       "userIdentity":{
4           "type":"IAMUser",
5           "principalId":"ABCDEFGHIJKL123456789",
6           "arn":"arn:aws:iam::123456789000:user/testuser",
7           "accountId":"123456789000",
8           "accessKeyId":"ABCDE12345EFGHIJKLMN",
9           "userName":"test user"
10      },
11      "eventTime":"2017-11-15T02:57:32Z",
12      "eventSource":"mediaconvert.amazonaws.com",
13      "eventName":"CreateJob",
14      "awsRegion":"us-west-2",
15      "sourceIPAddress":"1.2.3.4",
16      "userAgent":"PostmanRuntime/6.1.6",
17      "requestParameters":{
18          "settings":{
19              "outputGroups":[
20                  {
21                      "customName":"test",
22                      "name":"DASH ISO",
23                      "outputs":[
24                          {
25                              "containerSettings":{
26                                  "container":"MPD"
27                              },
28                              "videoDescription":{
29                                  "scalingBehavior":"DEFAULT",
30                                  "timecodeInsertion":"DISABLED",
31                                  "antiAlias":"ENABLED",
32                                  "sharpness":50,
33                                  "codecSettings":{
34                                      "codec":"H_264",
35                                      "h264Settings":{
36                                          "interlaceMode":"PROGRESSIVE",
37                                          "numberReferenceFrames":1,
38                                          "syntax":"DEFAULT",
39                                          "softness":0,
40                                          "gopClosedCadence":1,
41                                          "gopSize":90,
42                                          "slices":1,
43                                          "gopBReference":"DISABLED",
44                                          "slowPal":"DISABLED",
45                                          "spatialAdaptiveQuantization":"ENABLED",
46                                          "temporalAdaptiveQuantization":"ENABLED",
47                                          "flickerAdaptiveQuantization":"ENABLED",
48                                          "entropyEncoding":"CABAC",
49                                          "bitrate":5000000,
50                                          "framerateControl":"INITIALIZE_FROM_SOURCE",
```

```
51              "rateControlMode":"CBR",
52              "codecProfile":"MAIN",
53              "telecine":"NONE",
54              "minIInterval":0,
55              "adaptiveQuantization":"MEDIUM",
56              "codecLevel":"AUTO",
57              "fieldEncoding":"PAFF",
58              "sceneChangeDetect":"ENABLED",
59              "qualityTuningLevel":"SINGLE_PASS",
60              "framerateConversionAlgorithm":"DUPLICATE_DROP",
61              "unregisteredSeiTimecode":"DISABLED",
62              "gopSizeUnits":"FRAMES",
63              "parControl":"INITIALIZE_FROM_SOURCE",
64              "numberBFramesBetweenReferenceFrames":2,
65              "repeatPps":"DISABLED"
66            }
67          },
68          "afdSignaling":"NONE",
69          "dropFrameTimecode":"ENABLED",
70          "respondToAfd":"NONE",
71          "colorMetadata":"INSERT"
72        },
73        "audioDescriptions":[
74          {
75            "audioTypeControl":"FOLLOW_INPUT",
76            "codecSettings":{
77              "codec":"AAC",
78              "aacSettings":{
79                "audioDescriptionBroadcasterMix":"NORMAL",
80                "bitrate":96000,
81                "rateControlMode":"CBR",
82                "codecProfile":"LC",
83                "codingMode":"CODING_MODE_2_0",
84                "rawFormat":"NONE",
85                "sampleRate":48000,
86                "specification":"MPEG4"
87              }
88            },
89            "languageCodeControl":"FOLLOW_INPUT"
90          }
91        ],
92        "nameModifier":"aaa"
93      }
94    ],
95    "outputGroupSettings":{
96      "type":"DASH_ISO_GROUP_SETTINGS",
97      "dashIsoGroupSettings":{
98        "segmentLength":30,
99        "destination":"s3://testuser-testuser/clip01.mp4",
100       "encryption":"***",
101       "fragmentLength":2,
102       "segmentControl":"SINGLE_FILE",
103       "hbbtvCompliance":"NONE"
104     }
```

```
105                              }
106                          }
107                      ],
108                  "adAvailOffset":0,
109                  "inputs":[
110                      {
111                          "audioSelectors":{
112                              "Audio Selector 1":{
113                                  "offset":0,
114                                  "defaultSelection":"DEFAULT",
115                                  "programSelection":1
116                              }
117                          },
118                          "videoSelector":{
119                              "colorSpace":"FOLLOW"
120                          },
121                          "filterEnable":"AUTO",
122                          "psiControl":"USE_PSI",
123                          "filterStrength":0,
124                          "deblockFilter":"DISABLED",
125                          "denoiseFilter":"DISABLED",
126                          "timecodeSource":"EMBEDDED",
127                          "fileInput":"s3://mediaconvert-testuser/clip01.mp4"
128                      }
129                  ]
130              },
131          "role":"arn:aws:iam::123456789000:role/ecsInstanceRole",
132          "userMetadata":{
133              "Name":"Prod"
134          },
135          "queue":"arn:aws:mediaconvert:us-west-2:123456789000:queues/Default"
136      },
137      "responseElements":{
138          "job":{
139              "arn":"arn:aws:mediaconvert:us-west-2:123456789000:jobs/1510714652428-jyvx95",
140              "id":"1510714652428-jyvx95",
141              "createdAt":1510714652436,
142              "queue":"arn:aws:mediaconvert:us-west-2:123456789000:queues/Default",
143              "userMetadata":{
144                  "Name":"Prod"
145              },
146              "role":"arn:aws:iam::123456789000:role/ecsInstanceRole",
147              "settings":{
148                  "outputGroups":[
149                      {
150                          "customName":"test",
151                          "name":"DASH ISO",
152                          "outputs":[
153                              {
154                                  "containerSettings":{
155                                      "container":"MPD"
156                                  },
157                                  "videoDescription":{
158                                      "scalingBehavior":"DEFAULT",
```

```
159              "timecodeInsertion":"DISABLED",
160              "antiAlias":"ENABLED",
161              "sharpness":50,
162              "codecSettings":{
163                  "codec":"H_264",
164                  "h264Settings":{
165                      "interlaceMode":"PROGRESSIVE",
166                      "numberReferenceFrames":1,
167                      "syntax":"DEFAULT",
168                      "softness":0,
169                      "gopClosedCadence":1,
170                      "gopSize":90.0,
171                      "slices":1,
172                      "gopBReference":"DISABLED",
173                      "slowPal":"DISABLED",
174                      "spatialAdaptiveQuantization":"ENABLED",
175                      "temporalAdaptiveQuantization":"ENABLED",
176                      "flickerAdaptiveQuantization":"ENABLED",
177                      "entropyEncoding":"CABAC",
178                      "bitrate":5000000,
179                      "framerateControl":"INITIALIZE_FROM_SOURCE",
180                      "rateControlMode":"CBR",
181                      "codecProfile":"MAIN",
182                      "telecine":"NONE",
183                      "minIInterval":0,
184                      "adaptiveQuantization":"MEDIUM",
185                      "codecLevel":"AUTO",
186                      "fieldEncoding":"PAFF",
187                      "sceneChangeDetect":"ENABLED",
188                      "qualityTuningLevel":"SINGLE_PASS",
189                      "framerateConversionAlgorithm":"DUPLICATE_DROP",
190                      "unregisteredSeiTimecode":"DISABLED",
191                      "gopSizeUnits":"FRAMES",
192                      "parControl":"INITIALIZE_FROM_SOURCE",
193                      "numberBFramesBetweenReferenceFrames":2,
194                      "repeatPps":"DISABLED"
195                  }
196              },
197              "afdSignaling":"NONE",
198              "dropFrameTimecode":"ENABLED",
199              "respondToAfd":"NONE",
200              "colorMetadata":"INSERT"
201          },
202          "audioDescriptions":[
203              {
204                  "audioTypeControl":"FOLLOW_INPUT",
205                  "codecSettings":{
206                      "codec":"AAC",
207                      "aacSettings":{
208                          "audioDescriptionBroadcasterMix":"NORMAL",
209                          "bitrate":96000,
210                          "rateControlMode":"CBR",
211                          "codecProfile":"LC",
212                          "codingMode":"CODING_MODE_2_0",
```

```
213                         "rawFormat":"NONE",
214                         "sampleRate":48000,
215                         "specification":"MPEG4"
216                     }
217                 },
218                 "languageCodeControl":"FOLLOW_INPUT"
219             }
220         ],
221         "nameModifier":"aaa"
222     }
223 ],
224 "outputGroupSettings":{
225     "type":"DASH_ISO_GROUP_SETTINGS",
226     "dashIsoGroupSettings":{
227         "segmentLength":30,
228         "destination":"s3://mediaconvert-testuser/clip01.mp4",
229         "encryption":"***",
230         "fragmentLength":2,
231         "segmentControl":"SINGLE_FILE",
232         "hbbtvCompliance":"NONE"
233     }
234 }
235 }
236 ],
237 "adAvailOffset":0,
238 "inputs":[
239     {
240         "audioSelectors":{
241             "Audio Selector 1":{
242                 "offset":0,
243                 "defaultSelection":"DEFAULT",
244                 "programSelection":1
245             }
246         },
247         "videoSelector":{
248             "colorSpace":"FOLLOW"
249         },
250         "filterEnable":"AUTO",
251         "psiControl":"USE_PSI",
252         "filterStrength":0,
253         "deblockFilter":"DISABLED",
254         "denoiseFilter":"DISABLED",
255         "timecodeSource":"EMBEDDED",
256         "fileInput":"s3://mediaconvert-testuser/clip01.mp4"
257     }
258 ]
259 },
260 "status":"SUBMITTED",
261 "timing":{
262     "submitTime":"1510714652428"
263 }
264 }
265 },
266 "requestID":"b99d731e-c9b0-11e7-9b04-7fc9a0800896",
```

267   "eventID":"22ef8e82-ea2c-4014-9a45-16fd11474b31",
268   "readOnly":false,
269   "eventType":"AwsApiCall",
270   "recipientAccountId":"123456789000"
271 }

Document History for User Guide

The following table describes the documentation for this release of AWS Elemental MediaConvert.

- **API version: latest**
- **Latest documentation update:** November 27, 2017

Change	API version	Description	Date
New AWS Elemental MediaConvert service release		Initial documentation for the AWS Elemental MediaConvert service.	November 27, 2017

Note

The AWS Media Services are not designed or intended for use with applications or in situations requiring fail-safe performance, such as life safety operations, navigation or communication systems, air traffic control, or life support machines in which the unavailability, interruption or failure of the services could lead to death, personal injury, property damage or environmental damage. A component of AWS Elemental MediaConvert is licensed under the AVC patent portfolio license for the personal and non-commercial use of a consumer to (i) encode video in compliance with the AVC standard ("AVC video") and/or (ii) decode AVC video that was encoded by a consumer engaged in a personal and non-commercial activity and/or was obtained from a video provider licensed to provide AVC video. No license is granted or shall be implied for any other use. A component of AWS Elemental MediaConvert is licensed under the mpeg-4 patent portfolio license for the personal and non-commercial use of a consumer for (i) encoding video in compliance with the mpeg-4 visual standard ("mpeg-4 video") and/or (ii) decoding mpeg-4 video that was encoded by a consumer engaged in a personal and non-commercial activity and/or was obtained from a video provider licensed to provide AVC video. No license is granted or shall be implied for any other use. Additional information may be obtained from MPEG-LA, LLC. See http://www.mpegla.com. AWS Elemental MediaConvert may contain Dolby Digital and Dolby Digital Plus, which are protected under international and U.S. copyright laws as unpublished works. Dolby Digital and Dolby Digital Plus are confidential and proprietary to Dolby Laboratories. Their reproduction or disclosure, in whole or in part, or the production of derivative works therefrom without the express permission of Dolby Laboratories is prohibited. © Copyright 2003-2015 Dolby Laboratories. All rights reserved.

AWS Glossary

For the latest AWS terminology, see the AWS Glossary in the *AWS General Reference*.

www.ingramcontent.com/pod-product-compliance
Lightning Source LLC
LaVergne TN
LVHW082040050326
832904LV00005B/252